Nexus 7

FOR

DUMMIES®

Nexus 7™

FOR

DUMMIES®

by Dan Gookin

WILEY

John Wiley & Sons, Inc.

Nexus 7™ For Dummies®

Published by
John Wiley & Sons, Inc.
111 River Street
Hoboken, NJ 07030-5774

www.wiley.com

For general information on our other products and services, please contact our Customer Care Department within the U.S. at 877-762-2974, outside the U.S. at 317-572-3993, or fax 317-572-4002.

For technical support, please visit www.wiley.com/techsupport.

Wiley also publishes its books in a variety of electronic formats and by print-on-demand. Not all content that is available in standard print versions of this book may appear or be packaged in all book formats. If you have purchased a version of this book that did not include media that is referenced by or accompanies a standard print version, you may request this media by visiting http://booksupport.wiley.com. For more information about Wiley products, visit us www.wiley.com.

Library of Congress Control Number: 2012949141

ISBN 978-1-118-50873-2 (pbk); ISBN 978-1-118-51438-2 (ebk); ISBN 978-1-118-51441-2 (ebk); ISBN 978-1-118-50872-5 (ebk)

Manufactured in the United States of America

10 9 8 7 6 5 4 3

WILEY

About the Author

Dan Gookin has been writing about technology for over 25 years. He combines his love of writing with his gizmo fascination to create books that are informative, entertaining, and not boring. Having written over 130 titles with 12 million copies in print translated into over 30 languages, Dan can attest that his method of crafting computer tomes seems to work.

Perhaps his most famous title is the original *DOS For Dummies,* published in 1991. It became the world's fastest-selling computer book, at one time moving more copies per week than the *New York Times* number-one bestseller (though, as a reference, it could not be listed on the *Times'* Best Sellers list). That book spawned the entire line of *For Dummies* books, which remains a publishing phenomenon to this day.

Dan's most popular titles include *PCs For Dummies, Word For Dummies, Laptops For Dummies*, and *Android Phones For Dummies.* He also maintains the vast and helpful website www.wambooli.com.

Dan holds a degree in Communications/Visual Arts from the University of California, San Diego. He lives in the Pacific Northwest, where he enjoys spending time with his sons playing video games indoors while they enjoy the gentle woods of Idaho.

Publisher's Acknowledgments

We're proud of this book; please send us your comments at `http://dummies.custhelp.com`. For other comments, please contact our Customer Care Department within the U.S. at 877-762-2974, outside the U.S. at 317-572-3993, or fax 317-572-4002.

Some of the people who helped bring this book to market include the following:

Acquisitions and Editorial

Sr. Project Editor: Mark Enochs

Acquisitions Editor: Katie Mohr

Copy Editor: Rebecca Whitney

Editorial Manager: Leah Michael

Editorial Assistant: Leslie Saxman

Sr. Editorial Assistant: Cherie Case

Cover Photo: Background © beakraus/iStockphoto.com; image of phone provided by author

Cartoons: Rich Tennant (`www.the5thwave.com`)

Composition Services

Project Coordinator: Katie Crocker

Layout and Graphics: Carl Byers, Tim Detrick, Joyce Haughey, Christin Swinford

Proofreaders: John Greenough, Christine Sabooni

Indexer: Potomac Indexing, LLC

Publishing and Editorial for Technology Dummies

> **Richard Swadley,** Vice President and Executive Group Publisher
>
> **Andy Cummings,** Vice President and Publisher
>
> **Mary Bednarek,** Executive Acquisitions Director
>
> **Mary C. Corder,** Editorial Director

Publishing for Consumer Dummies

> **Kathy Nebenhaus,** Vice President and Executive Publisher

Composition Services

> **Debbie Stailey,** Director of Composition Services

Contents at a Glance

Table of Contents

Introduction

*W*elcome to the 21st century. Computers? Forget them! They're old, heavy, and clunky and not designed with the modern lifestyle in mind. Instead, you need to follow the trends and get a *tablet,* a mobile communications gizmo — something you can take with you and stay connected wherever you are.

Avoiding temptation to follow the trendy crowd, you've selected something unique. The Nexus 7 is not your normal tablet. It lacks a digital cellular connection and the monthly bills that come with it. It also lacks a rear-facing camera because, let's face it, tablets make lousy cameras. No, the Nexus 7 is truly different.

As a Nexus 7 owner, or someone who's interested in purchasing the device, you obviously want to get the most from your technology. It can be intimidating. It can be frustrating. No matter what, your experience can be made better by leisurely reading the book you have in your hands.

About This Book

This book was written to help you get the most from the Nexus 7's potential. It's a reference. Each chapter covers a specific topic, and the sections within each chapter address an issue related to the topic. Definitely, you don't have to read this book from front to back. In fact, I forbid you to do so.

The overall idea for this book is to show how things are done on the Nexus 7 and to help you get the most from the device without overwhelming you with information or intimidating you into despair.

Sample sections in this book include

- Locking the Nexus 7
- Activating voice input on the keyboard
- Importing contacts from your computer
- Setting up an Email account
- Running Facebook on your Nexus 7

✔ Talking and video chat

✔ Placing a Skype phone call

✔ Helping others find your location

✔ Flying with the Nexus 7

You have nothing to memorize, no sacred utterances or animal sacrifices, and definitely no PowerPoint presentations. Instead, every section explains a topic as though it's the first thing you read in this book. Nothing is assumed, and everything is cross-referenced. Technical terms and topics, when they come up, are neatly shoved to the side, where they're easily avoided. The idea here isn't to learn anything. This book's philosophy is to help you look it up, figure it out, and get on with your life.

How to Use This Book

This book follows a few conventions for using the Nexus 7. First of all, the Nexus 7 is referred to as the *Nexus 7* throughout the book. I might also refer to it as your *tablet,* for short.

Much of the material in this book applies to the Nexus 10 as well the Nexus 7, with just a few small differences. If you have a Nexus 10, you'll find this book just as useful as Nexus 7 users. So where I use *Nexus 7* in the text just pretend that you see *Nexus 10* instead.

The way you interact with the Nexus 7 is by using its *touchscreen,* the glassy part of the device as it's facing you. The device also has some physical buttons, as well as some holes and connectors. All these items are described in Chapter 1.

The various ways to touch the screen are explained and named in Chapter 2.

Chapter 3 discusses text input on the Nexus 7, which involves using an onscreen keyboard. You can also input text by speaking to the Nexus 7, which is also covered in Chapter 3.

This book directs you to do things by following numbered steps. Each step involves a specific activity, such as touching something on the screen; for example:

3. Choose Downloads.

This step directs you to touch the text or item labeled *Downloads* on the screen. You might also be told to do this:

3. Touch Downloads.

Some options can be turned off or on, as indicated by a gray box with a blue check mark in it, as shown in the margin. By touching the box on the screen, you add or remove the blue check mark. When the blue check mark appears, the option is on; otherwise, it's off.

Foolish Assumptions

Even though this book is written with the gentle hand-holding required by anyone who is just starting out, or who is easily intimidated, I've made a few assumptions. For example, I assume that you're a human being and not a colony creature from the planet Zontar.

My biggest assumption: You have a Nexus 7, manufactured by Asus and distributed by Google on the Internet as well as in various stores in the real world. As this book goes to press, the Nexus 7 has several variations depending on the internal memory capacity. There is also a cellular model, though its differences aren't enough to warrant separate coverage in this book.

I also assume that you have a computer, either a desktop or laptop. The computer can be a PC or Windows computer or a Macintosh. Oh, I suppose it could also be a Linux computer. In any event, I refer to your computer as *your computer* throughout this book. When directions are specific to a PC or Mac, the book says so.

Programs that run on the Nexus 7 are *apps*, which is short for *applications*. A single program is an app.

Finally, this book doesn't assume that you have a Google account, but already having one helps. Information is provided in Chapter 1 about setting up a Google account — an extremely important part of using the Nexus 7. Having a Google account opens up a slew of useful features, information, and programs that make using your tablet more productive.

How This Book Is Organized

This book is divided into five parts, each of which covers a certain aspect of the Nexus 7 or how it's used.

Part I: Introducing the Nexus 7

This part of the book covers setup and orientation to familiarize you with how the device works. It's a good place to start if you're completely new to the concept of tablet computing, mobile devices, or the Android operating system.

Part II: Keep in Touch

In this part of the book, you read about various ways that the Nexus 7 can electronically communicate with your online friends. There's texting, e-mail, the web, social networking, and even the much-wanted trick of using the non-phone Nexus 7 to make phone calls and do video chat.

Part III: But Wait — There's More!

The Nexus 7 is pretty much a limitless gizmo. To prove it, the chapters in this part of the book cover all the various and wonderful things the tablet does: It's an eBook reader, a map, a navigator, a photo album, a portable music player, a calendar, a calculator, and potentially much more.

Part IV: Nuts and Bolts

Part IV of this book covers a lot of different topics. Up first is how to connect the Nexus 7 wirelessly to the Internet as well as to other gizmos, such as a Bluetooth printer. There's a chapter on sharing and exchanging files with your computer. Then come the maintenance, customization, and troubleshooting chapters.

Part V: The Part of Tens

Things are wrapped up in this book with the traditional *For Dummies* Part of Tens. Each chapter in this part lists ten items or topics. The chapters include tips, tricks, shortcuts, things to remember, and things not to forget — plus, a smattering of useful apps that no Nexus 7 should be without.

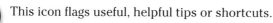

Icons Used in This Book

This icon flags useful, helpful tips or shortcuts.

This icon marks a friendly reminder to do something.

This icon marks a friendly reminder not to do something.

This icon alerts you to overly nerdy information and technical discussions of the topic at hand. Reading the information is optional, though it may win you the Daily Double on *Jeopardy!*

Where to Go from Here

Start reading! Observe the table of contents and find something that interests you. Or look up your puzzle in the index. When these suggestions don't cut it, just start reading Chapter 1.

My e-mail address is dgookin@wambooli.com. Yes, that's my real address. I reply to all e-mail I get, and you'll get a quick reply if you keep your question short and specific to this book. Although I do enjoy saying Hi, I cannot answer technical support questions, resolve billing issues, or help you troubleshoot your Nexus 7. Thanks for understanding.

You can also visit my web page for more information or as a diversion: www.wambooli.com. Specific support for the Nexus 7 is found here on my website: www.wambooli.com/help/tablets/ nexus7.

Enjoy this book and your Nexus 7!

Part I
Introducing the Nexus 7

The 5th Wave   By Rich Tennant

"What I'm doing should clear your sinuses, take away your headache, and charge your Nexus 7."

In this part . . .

After several thousand years, tablets are once again all the rage. Babylonians wrote on them. Moses brought them down from Mount Sinai. Ancient Roman schoolboys did their homework on them. Tablets are nothing new.

Then again, those ancient tablets aren't really the same as modern mobile computing devices. Ancient tablets didn't use batteries. They didn't communicate wirelessly with the Internet. They didn't let you update your social networking status, read books, play music, find tacos, or do any of the wonderful things a modern tablet is capable of. So maybe the Nexus 7 is something new and different. Consider this part of the book your introduction to the 21st century tablet.

Chapter 1

Behold the Nexus

. . . .

In This Chapter

▷ Unboxing your Nexus 7

▷ Charging the battery

▷ Locating important things

▷ Setting up and configuring the tablet

▷ Unlocking the screen

▷ Controlling lock time-out

▷ Shutting down the Nexus 7

▷ Storing your tablet

. . . .

*Y*our tablet adventures with the Nexus 7 begin by opening its box. Sure, you've probably already done that. I don't blame you: I opened the box and played with my Nexus 7 before I read this chapter, too. No problem. To help you relive the experience, or to get yourself oriented if you found the experience daunting — or to simply prepare you for that out-of-the-box experience yet to come — this chapter provides you with a gentle introduction to your new Google tablet, the Nexus 7.

Nexus 7 Setup

Fortunately, setting up your Nexus 7 tablet isn't complex or time-consuming. It doesn't bother gathering a goat and waiting for a full moon, nor do you need to hire a man with a long beard and pointy hat. You pretty much have to liberate the tablet, assemble it, charge the battery, and then set up your Google account. That's it.

Well, yeah, I can write "That's it," but obviously the process can be intimidating. This section offers some pointers.

Liberating your tablet

The Nexus 7 works best outside of its box: Lift the device from its container, and merrily remove the plastic sheeting that cocoons the gizmo. Root around inside the box, and locate the following items:

✓ **A USB cable:** You can use it to connect the Nexus 7 to a computer or a wall charger.

✓ **A wall charger:** Use this thing to charge the tablet. The USB cable plugs into the wall charger, and then it connects to the Nexus 7, as described in the next section.

✓ **Useless pamphlets:** Two booklets come with the Nexus 7 — a warranty that you can avoid reading and a *Quick Start Guide,* which is heavy on the quick and light on the guide.

✓ **Golden Ticket:** Rumor has it that five of the millions of Nexus 7s out there come with a special Golden Ticket. The winners receive a tour of Google's secret facilities and a lifetime supply of Wi-Fi.

Keep the box for as long as you own your Nexus 7. If you ever need to return the thing or ship it somewhere, the original box is the ideal container. You can shove the useless pamphlets back into the box as well.

Your Nexus 7 isn't limited to the paltry assortment of items included in the box. There exists a bounty of additional goodies you can get for your tablet, including earbud-style earphones for listening to music; a headset for making phone calls; a car charger for taking the tablet on the road; numerous handsome carrying cases; and other assorted goodies. You can find these accessories at the Google Play Store on the Internet, at other various online vendors, or wherever you purchased the tablet.

Charging the battery

The first thing that I recommend you do with your Nexus 7 is give it a full charge. Obey these steps:

1. Connect the USB cable to the wall adapter.

The cable plugs in only one way.

2. **Connect the other end of the USB cable to the Nexus 7.**

   The cable attaches to the bottom of the tablet. Again, it plugs in only one way.

3. **Plug the wall adapter into the wall.**

Upon success, you may see a large battery-charging icon appear on the touchscreen. Yes, it happens even though the Nexus 7 isn't turned on yet. The battery-charging icon lets you know that the Nexus 7 is functioning properly, though you shouldn't be alarmed if it fails to appear.

🖛 Your Nexus 7 most likely comes partially charged from the factory, though I still recommend giving it an initial charge, just in case, as well as to familiarize yourself with the process.

🖛 The USB cable is used for charging the Nexus 7 and for connecting it to a computer to share information or exchange files. (Read more about exchanging files in Chapter 14.)

🖛 You can also charge the Nexus 7 by connecting it to a computer's USB port. As long as the computer is on, the tablet charges. Even so:

🖛 The battery charges more efficiently if you plug it into a wall rather than charge it from a computer's USB port.

🖛 The Nexus 7 doesn't feature a removable battery.

Setting up your Nexus 7

The final act of getting your new tablet ready for use is to tell it a bit about yourself. Specifically, you need to coordinate your Google account with the tablet. Doing so gives you mobile access to your Gmail, Calendar, YouTube, and other, myriad Google accounts. Further, you need to set up some other tablet features, such as your language, the Wi-Fi networking connection, and location services.

If initial setup was already done for you by the friendly salespeople where you bought your Nexus 7, you're good to go. Skip on over to the next section. Otherwise, the account setup adventure begins by turning on the Nexus 7 for the first time. Heed these directions:

1. **Press the Power Lock button.**

   You may have to press it longer than you think. When you see the text *Google* appear on the screen, the Nexus 7 has started. (You can release the button.)

2. **Unlock the Nexus by dragging the Unlock button out toward the unlocking ring, as shown in Figure 1-1.**

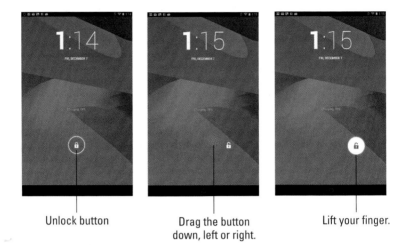

Unlock button   Drag the button   Lift your finger.
down, left or right.

Figure 1-1: Unlock the Nexus 7.

To drag the button, touch it with your finger. Keep your finger on the touchscreen and drag up, down, left, or right, as illustrated in Figure 1-1. The unlocking ring doesn't appear until you move the Unlock button. Lift your finger when the Unlock button changes, as shown in the figure.

Normally when you unlock the Nexus 7, you can start doing things. (That discussion comes later.) Because you're starting the tablet for the first time, you have to run through the setup process. The first thing to do is to tell the Nexus 7 which language to use.

3. **Optionally, choose your language.**

On my tablet's screen, it says *English (United States)*. If you need to change the language, touch the Menu triangle (shown in the margin, and found in the lower-right corner of the Language button) to choose another language.

4. **Touch the Big Triangle button to proceed.**

The triangle button is shown in the margin.

The next step is to set up the Wi-Fi connection.

5. **Choose a Wi-Fi network.**

Assuming that a Wi-Fi network is in range, select it on the screen. Or when you see multiple Wi-Fi networks available, pick the one you use most often. On my screen, I chose the Imperial Wambooli network, my local wireless network.

When the Wi-Fi network name doesn't show up, touch the Plus (+) button at the bottom of the screen, next to the text *Other Network*. Also see Chapter 13 for information on connecting to Wi-Fi networks. You can always add more Wi-Fi networks later, so skipping this step is okay.

6. **Type the password using the keyboard that appears on the screen.**

   Chapter 3 covers using the onscreen keyboard.

7. **Touch the Connect button.**

   Watch in amazement as the tablet connects to the wireless network.

   The next step is to configure your Google account, associating it with the Nexus 7. If you don't yet have a Google account, get one! See the "**Get yourself a Google account!**" sidebar, later in this chapter.

8. **If necessary, obey the directions on the screen to sign in to your Google account; fill in the information as prompted.**

   This step may not be necessary, if you already have a Google account and use Google for your mobile devices. In this case, Google may instantly recognize you (which is pretty amazing) and identify your Google account. If so, type your Gmail password, and then touch the big triangle to log in to your Gmail account.

9. **At the Backup and Restore Screen, ensure that both options are selected, and then touch the Big Triangle button to continue.**

   Information from your Google account is then synchronized with the Nexus 7, including contacts, calendars, YouTube information, bookmarks from the Chrome browser, and a host of other goodies.

   The next, and final, step is to specify which location services the tablet uses.

10. **Ensure that all check boxes for the location services are selected.**

    The location services help the Nexus 7 locate wherever you are on Planet Earth. They're used for navigating, finding locations, checking out people near you, and engaging in other fun activities. I highly recommend that you activate the location services.

11. **Touch the Big Triangle to continue.**

    Setup is complete.

12. **Touch the Big Triangle to start using your Nexus 7.**

Get yourself a Google account!

If you don't already have a Google account, run — don't walk or mince — to a computer and create your own, free Google account: Use the computer's web browser program to visit the main Google page, www.google.com. On that page, click the Sign In button or link. If you don't see *Sign In*, you already have a Google account. You're done.

After you click the Sign In button, another page appears. Locate the button or link that lets you create a new account. As this book goes to press, the button is labeled Sign Up, though it may change in the future. Continue heeding the directions on the screen until you've created your own Google account.

After your account is set up and configured. I recommend that you log off and then log back on to Google, just to ensure that you did everything properly.

These directions may change subtly, depending on updates to the Nexus 7 software. Even if you skip an option, you can always review and change your choices by using the Settings app, as described throughout this book.

✐ The setup process works differently when you have a Nexus 7 that can access the digital cellular network. In addition to the steps in this section, you must also activate the tablet, ensuring that it has a Network ID number. That way you can get all those wonderful monthly cellular bills.

✐ If you're lucky, you may get a Google Play gift certificate after completing the setup process. Refer to Chapter 12 for information on Google Play and how to use your credit.

✐ And you thought I was kidding about the Golden Ticket.

Know Your Gizmo

"Second star to the right and straight on till morning" may get Peter Pan to Neverland, but for navigating your way around the Nexus 7, you need more specific directions.

Take heed of Figure 1-2, which is my attempt at illustrating the basic Nexus 7 hardware features. Follow along on your own tablet as you find key features, described in this section.

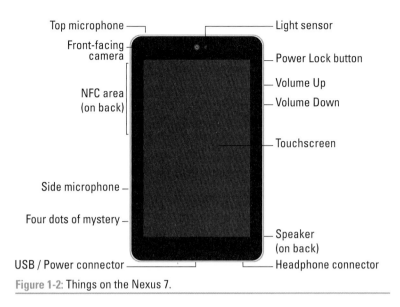

Figure 1-2: Things on the Nexus 7.

Power Lock: The Power Lock button appears on the upper-right side of the Nexus 7. It's more toward the back of the tablet than on its side. You use the Power Lock button to turn the Nexus 7 on or off or to lock the touchscreen, as described later in this chapter.

Volume Up/Volume Down: To control the volume on your tablet, use the Volume button found on the right side of the Nexus 7. It's one button but two switches. Press the top part to increase the volume; press the bottom part to lower the volume.

Touchscreen: The biggest part of the Nexus 7 is its touchscreen display, which occupies a goodly chunk of real estate on the front of the device. The touchscreen display is a see-touch thing: You look at it and also touch it with your fingers to control the tablet.

Speaker: The Nexus 7's speaker appears as a long, thin slit that's parallel to the bottom edge of the device, found on the back.

Headphone connector: At the bottom right edge, just next to the USB / Power connector, you see a hole where you can connect standard headphones.

USB / Power connector: At the bottom center of your Nexus 7, almost like a drain hole, is the USB / Power connector. That's where you attach the USB cable to charge the tablet but also to connect to a computer for exchanging files.

Four dots of mystery: Officially, it's known as the 4-pin connector although the term *pogo pins* is also used. The dots are used for communications between the tablet and a docking station.

Microphone: The Nexus 7 has two microphones, both of which appear as tiny holes in the case. One is found on the top, and the other on the device's left side, as shown in Figure 1-2.

NFC area: Found on the upper back of the tablet (though not clearly identifiable), the Near Field Communications area allows the Nexus 7 to communicate wirelessly with other NFC devices. See Chapter 13 for details.

Front camera: The Nexus 7's front-facing camera is centered above the touchscreen. The camera is used for taking self-portraits as well as for video conferencing.

Light sensor: Though it's difficult to see, just to the right of the front camera is a teensy light sensor. It's used to help adjust the brightness level of the touchscreen.

Using these various doodads, holes, and buttons is covered throughout this book. Chapter 2 touches upon using the device itself.

✔ Don't stick anything into the microphone hole! Yeah, it's about the size of an unbent paper clip, so avoid the temptation. The only things you need to stick into the Nexus 7 are the USB cable and headphones.

✔ The Power Lock button cannot be accidentally pressed while the Nexus 7 is lying flat on a table. You have to lift the tablet before you can press the button.

It's a Turn-On

There should be nothing more simple than turning on a device. That's probably based on years of electrically powered gizmos that featured the clever and innovative "on–off" switch. Well, those days are long gone.

Today's electronics feature a power button. It's called a *power* button because it no longer serves as the simple on–off switch. It does more, depending on the device's mood. Therefore, the simple process of turning on something like the Nexus 7 requires some detailed explanation, which you find in this section.

Turning on your Nexus 7

To turn on your Nexus 7, press and hold the Power Lock button. After a few seconds, you see the word *Google* appear on the touchscreen. It means that the tablet has started and that you can release the Power Lock button.

After the Nexus 7 has been turned on, the next step is usually to unlock the device. This process is covered in the next section.

✔ Refer to Figure 1-2 for the specific location of the Power Lock button.

✔ You need to work through some initial setup the first time you turn on your Nexus 7. See the earlier section "Setting up your Nexus 7."

✔ You probably won't turn on your Nexus 7 much in the future. Mostly, you simply unlock the device.

Unlocking the Nexus 7

You'll probably leave your Nexus 7 on all the time. It was designed that way. The battery lasts quite a while, so when the tablet is bored or when you've ignored it for a while, it falls asleep, locking itself and turning off the screen to save power.

To unlock the Nexus 7, press the Power Lock button. Unlike turning on the tablet, a quick press of the Power Lock button is all that's needed.

After unlocking the Nexus 7, you may see the lock screen. The various lock screens are illustrated in Figure 1-1. There's also the possibility that the tablet may not even have a lock screen. See Chapter 16 for information on setting up this option (though I don't recommend it).

✔ Information on the additional lock screens is covered in the next section.

✔ Also see the later section "Locking the Nexus 7."

  ✔ If music is playing while the Nexus 7 is locked, the lock screen
    shows a preview of the album art as well as controls for
    manipulating the music. See Chapter 10 for more information
    on using your tablet to play music.

Working the various lock screens

The standard unlock screen on the Nexus 7 isn't a tough lock to
pick. Therefore, other lock screens may appear, which offer
different levels of security for your tablet.

Figure 1-3 illustrates the four locking screens that are possible with
the Nexus 7.

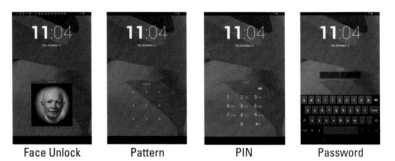

| Face Unlock | Pattern | PIN | Password |

Figure 1-3: More sophisticated ways to unlock the Nexus 7.

To work the Face Unlock feature, stare at the Nexus 7 after you
press the Power Lock button. If your punim matches, you can start
using the tablet. Otherwise, you're prompted with a pattern or PIN
lock as a backup.

The pattern lock requires that you trace your finger along a pattern
that includes as many as nine dots on the screen. After you match
the pattern, the Nexus 7 is unlocked, and you can start using it.

The PIN lock requires that you type a secret number to unlock the
Nexus 7. Touch the Enter button (the arrow button in the lower-
right corner of the keypad) to accept input, or use the Del button
(shown in the margin) to back up and erase.

Finally, the password lock requires that you type a multicharacter
password on the screen before the Nexus 7 is unlocked. To type
your password, touch the text box in the center of the unlock

screen to summon the onscreen keyboard. Type the password. Touch the Done button to accept the password and unlock the Nexus 7.

- ✔ Whether or not you see these various lock screens depends on how you've configured the Nexus 7's security. Specific directions for setting the locks, or for removing them and returning to the standard screen lock, are found in Chapter 16.

- ✔ The password lock must contain at least one letter and number, though it can also include a smattering of symbols and other characters.

- ✔ For additional information on working the onscreen keyboard, see Chapter 3.

Who is this Android person?

Just like your computer, your Nexus 7 has an *operating system.* It's the main program in charge of all the software (other programs or *apps*) inside the tablet. Unlike on your computer, however, Android is a *mobile device* operating system, designed for use in cell phones and tablets. It's because of this dual nature that you often see the Nexus 7 referred to as a "device" on the various settings screens.

You find the Android operating system used on many of today's most popular smartphones as well as on a whole lineup of tablets. By using Android, the Nexus 7 has access to all the Android software — the apps— available to Android mobile devices. You can read how to add these apps to your tablet in Chapter 12.

Android is based on the Linux operating system, which is also a computer operating system, though it's much more stable and bugfree than Windows, so it's not as popular. Google owns, maintains, and develops Android, which is why your online Google information is synced with the Nexus 7.

The Android mascot, shown here, often appears in Android apps or hardware. He has no official name, though most folks call him Andy.

It's a Turn-Off

I know of three ways to say goodbye to your Nexus 7, and only one of them involves a steamroller. The other two methods are documented in this section.

Locking the Nexus 7

The most common way to dismiss your Nexus 7 is to lock it: Press the Power Lock button. The display goes dark; the tablet is locked.

▸ The Nexus 7 still works while it's locked: It still receives e-mail, and it can still play music. But it's not using as much power as it would when the touchscreen is on.

▸ Your Nexus 7 will probably spend most of its time locked.

▸ Locking doesn't turn off the Nexus 7.

▸ Any timers or alarms you set still activate when the tablet is locked. See Chapter 11 for information on setting alarms.

▸ To unlock the Nexus 7, press and release the Power Lock button. See the section "Unlocking the Nexus 7," earlier in this chapter.

Controlling the lock time-out

You can manually lock the Nexus 7 at any time by pressing the Power Lock button. That's why it's called the Power *Lock* button. When you don't manually lock, the tablet automatically locks itself after a given period of inactivity. How long? That's up to you, though the Nexus 7 is preconfigured to *snooze* (self-lock) after ten minutes of your ignoring it.

To set the time-out to something other than ten minutes, obey these steps:

1. **At the Home screen, touch the All Apps button.**

2. **Choose Settings to open the Settings app.**

3. **Choose Display and then Sleep.**

4. **Choose a time-out value from the Sleep menu.**

   The range is from 15 seconds to 30 minutes at various intervals. I prefer 1 minute.

5. **Touch the Home button to return to the Home screen.**

The lock timer begins after a period of inactivity, when you don't touch the screen or the timer starts ticking. About five seconds before the time-out value you set (refer to Step 4), the touchscreen dims. Then it turns off and the screen locks. If you touch the screen before then, the timer is reset.

🖝 Also see Chapter 16 for information on setting whether the Nexus 7 locks immediately after sleeping or after a delay.

🖝 Chapter 18 discusses the Stay Awake setting, where the tablet doesn't sleep as long as it's connected to a power source.

Turning off the Nexus 7

To turn off your tablet gizmo, heed these steps:

1. Press and hold the Power Lock button.

You see the Device Options menu, shown in Figure 1-4.

⏻ Power off

✈ Airplane mode
Airplane mode is OFF

🔊 Silent mode
Sound is ON

Figure 1-4: The Device Options menu.

If you chicken out and don't want to turn off the Nexus 7, touch the Back icon button to dismiss the Device Options menu.

2. Touch the Power Off item.

3. Touch OK.

The Nexus 7 turns itself off.

The tablet doesn't run when it's off, so it doesn't remind you of appointments, collect e-mail, or let you hear any alarms you've set. Neither is the Nexus 7 angry with you for turning it off, though you may sense some resentment when you turn it on again.

Be sure to keep the Nexus in a safe place while it's turned off. See the next section.

Where to Keep Your Nexus 7

As with your car keys, glasses, wallet, and samovar, keep your Nexus 7 in a place where it's safe, easy to find, and always handy whether you're at home, at work, or on the road.

I recommend storing the Nexus 7 in the same spot when you're done using it. My first suggestion is to make a spot next to your computer. Keep the charging cord handy, or simply plug the cord into the computer's USB port so that you can synchronize information with your computer regularly and keep the tablet charged.

✔ Avoid keeping the Nexus 7 in a place where someone might sit on it, step on it, or damage it. For example, don't leave the tablet under a stack of newspapers on a table or counter, where it might get accidentally tossed out or put in the recycle bin.

✔ The ideal storage spot for the Nexus 7 is a specially designed carrying case or pouch, such as the type of pouches mama kangaroos have, but without the expense of owning a zoo.

✔ A desktop docking station also makes a great storage place for the Nexus 7.

✔ As long as you remember to return the tablet to the same spot when you're done with it, you'll always know where it is.

Chapter 2

How It Works

*W*here are the buttons? The knobs? The dials? If the Nexus 7 is so advanced, how do you control the thing?

Oh, don't fret: You have many ways to manipulate your tablet. Primarily, the Nexus 7 uses a touchscreen interface. It more than makes up for the lack of buttons. You use the touchscreen to control the tablet, which is probably a new experience for you. If not, you can appreciate this chapter as a quick review of how to use your Nexus 7's basic features.

Basic Operations

The first baby steps toward learning how to manipulate the Nexus 7 are truly simple. The terminology is most definitely not simple. This section helps iron things out.

Touching the screen

Minus buttons, knobs, and dials, you have to rely upon the touchscreen to control your Nexus 7. To make the touchscreen work, you have to touch it. Yes, that means disregarding all those admonitions from when you were young not to touch the TV or the front of the oven. When it comes to using the Nexus 7, touching is everything.

You touch the screen using one or more of your fingers. It doesn't matter which fingers you use, and you can probably use the tip of your nose as well, though I leave that up to you.

Here are the many ways the touchscreen can be touched:

Touch: The simplest way to manipulate the touchscreen is to touch it. You touch an object, an icon, a control, a menu item, a doodad, and so on. The touch operation is similar to a mouse click on a computer. It may also be referred to as a *tap* or *press.*

Double-tap: Touch the screen twice in the same location. Double-tapping can be used to zoom in on an image or a map, but it can also zoom out. Because of the double-tap's dual nature, I recommend using the *pinch* or *spread* operation instead when you want to zoom.

Long-press: A long-press occurs when you touch part of the screen and hold your finger down. Depending on what you're doing, a pop-up menu may appear, or the item you're long-pressing may get "picked up" so that you can drag (move) it around after a long-press. *Long-press* might also be referred to as *touch and hold* in some documentation.

Swipe: To swipe, you touch your finger on one spot and then drag it to another spot. Swipes can go up, down, left, or right, which moves the touchscreen content in the direction you swipe your finger. A swipe can be fast or slow. It's also called a *flick* or *slide.*

Pinch: A pinch involves two fingers, which start out separated and then are brought together. The effect is used to *zoom out,* to reduce the size of an image or see more of a map.

Spread: The opposite of *pinch* is *spread.* You start out with your fingers together and then spread them. The spread is used to *zoom in,* to enlarge an image or see more detail on a map.

Rotate: A few apps let you rotate an image on the screen by touching with two fingers and twisting them around a center point. Think of turning a combination lock on a safe, and you get the rotate operation.

You can't manipulate the touchscreen while wearing gloves unless they're gloves specially designed for using electronic touch-screens, such as the gloves that Batman wears.

Also see Chapter 17 for recommendations on properly cleaning the touchscreen, which must be done inevitably.

Changing the orientation

The Nexus 7 features a gizmo called an *accelerometer*. It determines in which direction the tablet is pointed or whether you've reoriented the device from an upright to a horizontal position, or even upside down. That way, the information on the tablet always appears upright, no matter how you hold it.

To demonstrate how the Nexus 7 orients itself, follow these steps:

1. **At the Home screen, touch the All Apps button.**

   The All Apps screen appears. (It's covered later in this chapter.)

2. **Touch the Chrome icon.**

   The Chrome app starts. It's the tablet's web browser.

3. **Turn the Nexus 7 to the left or right so that it's in the horizontal orientation.**

   The display rotates to properly orient the screen content, as illustrated in Figure 2-1.

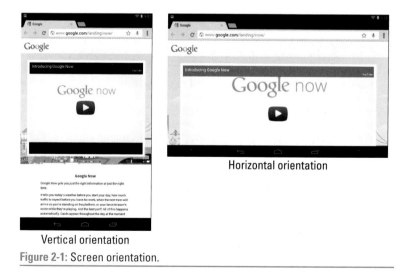

Horizontal orientation

Vertical orientation

Figure 2-1: Screen orientation.

Most apps change their orientation to match however you've turned the tablet, such as the Chrome app, shown in Figure 2-1.

But the rotation feature may not work for all apps, such as certain games and older Android apps.

✔ The screen can rotate left, right, or even upside down.

✔ You can lock the orientation if the rotating screen bothers you. See the section "Setting quick options," later in this chapter.

✔ A great application for demonstrating the Nexus 7 accelerometer is the game *Labyrinth*. It can be purchased at the Google Play Store, or the free version, *Labyrinth Lite,* can be downloaded. See Chapter 12 for more information about the Google Play Store.

Controlling the volume

Sometimes the sound level is too loud. Sometimes it's too soft. And rarely, the sound is just right. Finding that just-right level is the job of the volume-control buttons that cling to the right side of the Nexus 7.

Pressing the top part of the Volume button makes the volume louder; pressing the bottom part makes the volume softer. As you press the button, a graphic appears on the touchscreen to illustrate the relative volume level, as shown in Figure 2-2.

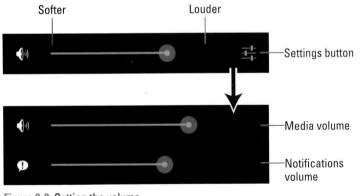

Figure 2-2: Setting the volume.

Touch the Settings button, shown in Figure 2-2, to see more-detailed volume controls. You can set the volume for media and notifications individually, as shown in the expanded onscreen volume control: Drag the blue dot left or right to set the volume.

🖝 When the volume is set all the way down, the Nexus 7 is silenced.

🖝 Silencing the tablet by sliding down the volume level places it into Vibration mode.

🖝 The Volume button works even when the tablet is locked. That means you don't need to wake the tablet if you're playing music and need to adjust the volume.

🖝 A third slider is available for alarms, though it doesn't show up in the expanded volume control. (Refer to Figure 2-2.) See Chapter 16.

There's No Place Like Home Screen

The main base from which you begin your exploration of the Nexus 7 is the *Home* screen. It's the first thing you see after unlocking the tablet, and it's the place you go to whenever you quit an app.

Touring the Home screen

A typical Nexus 7 Home screen is illustrated in Figure 2-3.

Here are several fun and interesting things to notice on the Home screen:

Notification icons: These icons come and go, depending on what happens in your digital life. For example, new icons appear whenever you receive a new e-mail message or have a pending appointment. The later section "Reviewing notifications" describes how to deal with notifications.

Status icons: These icons represent the Nexus 7's current condition, such as its battery status or Wi-Fi network signal strength or whether an alarm is set or Bluetooth is active, for example.

Widgets: A *widget* is a teensy program that can display information, let you control the tablet, access features, or do something purely amusing. You can read more about widgets in Chapter 16. Google Now widgets are covered in Chapter 11.

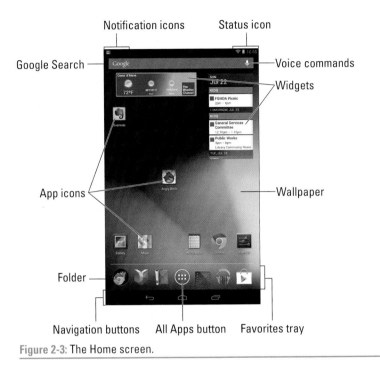

Notification icons   Status icon

Google Search ——   ——Voice commands

                                                        ╱Widgets

App icons   ——Wallpaper

Folder ——

Navigation buttons   All Apps button   Favorites tray

Figure 2-3: The Home screen.

App icons: These little pictures represent the apps (applications) installed on your tablet. They're stuck on the Home screen for convenient access. Touching an app icon opens, or runs, the app.

Wallpaper: The background image you see on the Home screen is the wallpaper. It can be changed, as described in Chapter 18.

All Apps button: Near the bottom center of the Home screen is the All Apps button. Touching this button displays the All Apps screen, which lists all apps installed on your Nexus 7. See the later section "Visiting the All Apps screen" for details.

Favorites Tray: The lineup of icons near the bottom of the screen contains six slots for popular apps. They can appear singularly or in folders, as illustrated earlier, in Figure 2-3. Chapter 16 explains how to add or remove apps from the Favorites bar as well as how to create folders.

Navigation buttons: Special symbols are found at the bottom center of the Home screen as well as in quite a few apps. The symbols identify buttons you touch to activate common Nexus 7 features.

Ensure that you recognize the names of the various parts of the Home screen, because the terms are used throughout this book and in whatever other scant Nexus 7 documentation exists.

✓ The Home screen shown earlier, in Figure 2-3, is not the preconfigured Home screen that comes with the Nexus 7. That's because:

✓ The Home screen is entirely customizable. You can add and remove icons from the Home screen, add widgets, build app folders, and even change wallpaper (background) images. See Chapter 16 for more information.

✓ Touching a part of the Home screen that doesn't feature an icon or a control does nothing. That is, unless you're using the *live wallpaper* feature. In that case, touching the screen changes the wallpaper in some way, depending on the wallpaper that's selected. You can read more about live wallpaper in Chapter 16.

Accessing multiple Home screens

The Home screen is more than what you see. It's actually an entire street of Home screens, with only one Home screen *panel* displayed at a time.

To switch from one panel to another, swipe the Home screen left or right. Two panels dwell to the left of the main Home screen panel, and two panels to the right.

When you touch the Home navigation button, you return to the last Home screen panel you viewed. To return to the main, center Home screen panel, touch the Home icon button a second time.

Using the icon buttons

Anchoring the bottom of the Nexus 7 Home screen are three common icon buttons, called *navigation buttons.* These buttons are used to control the tablet, considering that the device lacks the necessary physical buttons. Table 2-1 lists the navigation buttons and their functions.

Table 2-1		Navigation Buttons
Button	*Name*	*What It Does*
⬅	Back	Goes back, closes, or dismisses the onscreen keyboard
⌂	Home	Goes to the Home screen
▢	Recent	Displays recently opened apps
⌄	Hide	Dismisses the onscreen keyboard
●	Dot	Appears when the buttons are available but hidden

The navigation buttons listed in Table 2-1 are found at the bottom of the screen almost all the time. Sometimes they may be dimmed or hidden, replaced with a faint dot. In that case, touch the dot replacing the navigation button to activate its feature.

The navigation buttons always appear in the order Back, Home, and Recent.

In addition to the navigation buttons, you find other common icon buttons and symbols used on the Nexus 7. Table 2-2 lists the most common icon buttons and the tasks they do.

Table 2-2		Common Icon Buttons
Button	*Name*	*What It Does*
	Add	Adds or creates a new item. The plus symbol (+) may be used in combination with other symbols, depending on the app.
	Close	Closes a window or clears text from an input field.
	Dictation	Lets you use your voice to dictate text. On the Home screen, dictation is used with the Google Search function.
	Edit	Lets you edit an item, add text, or fill in fields.
	Expand	Enlarges the app to fill the screen.
	Favorite	Flags a favorite item, such as a contact or web page.
	Menu	Displays the menu for an app. This icon button is often found in the upper-right corner of the screen, though occasionally it shows up in the lower-right corner.
	Menu button	Displays a pop-up menu. This teensy icon appears in the lower-right corner of a button.
	Refresh	Fetches new information or reloads.

(continued)

Table 2-2 *(continued)*

Button	Name	What It Does
	Search	Searches the Nexus 7 or the Internet for a tidbit of information.
	Settings	Adjusts options for an app.
	Share	Shares information stored on the tablet via e-mail, social networking, or other Internet services.
	Sync	Synchronizes information, such as updating data shared on the Internet.

Various sections throughout this book give examples of using the icon buttons. Their images appear in the book's margins wherever relevant.

Common Activities

To become a cat, you must know how to perform several duties: sleep, eat, catch critters, and cause mischief. A cat's life isn't difficult, and neither is your Nexus 7 life, as long as you know how to do some basic duties on the Home screen. Like the cat, you have only a few duties to know about.

Starting an app

It's blissfully simple to run an app on the Home screen: Touch its icon. The app starts.

> ✓ Not all apps appear on the Home screen, but all of them appear when you display the All Apps screen. See the section "Visiting the All Apps screen," later in this chapter.

> ✓ When an app closes or you quit the app, you're returned to the Home screen.

> ✓ App is short for *application*. It's another word for *program* or *software*.

Working a widget

Like app icons, widgets appear on the Home screen. To use a widget, touch it. What happens next depends, of course, on the widget and what it does.

For example, the YouTube widget lets you peruse videos like you're flipping the pages in a book. Touch a video to view it.

Other widgets do interesting things, display useful information, or give you access to the Nexus 7's features.

> ✓ See Chapter 16 for details on adding widgets to the Home screen.

> ✓ Widgets are downloaded like apps. See Chapter 12, about the Google Play Store.

Reviewing notifications

Notifications appear as icons at the upper-left corner of the Home screen, as illustrated earlier, in Figure 2-3. To review them, you pull down the notifications shade by dragging your finger from the top left part of the screen to the bottom. The notifications shade is illustrated in Figure 2-4.

Drag down from here
to see notifications.

Dismiss all
notifications.

Swipe a notification to
the right to dismiss it.

Choose a notification
to see more details.

Notification shade
handle

Notifications

Figure 2-4: Perusing notifications.

Touch a notification to deal with it. What happens next depends on the notification, but most often the app that generated the notification appears. You might also be given the opportunity to deal with whatever caused the notification, such as a calendar appointment.

Individual notifications are dismissed by sliding them to the right, as illustrated in Figure 2-4.

To dismiss all notifications, touch the Dismiss All button. (Refer to Figure 2-4.)

When you're done looking, you can slide the notifications shade up again: Touch the notifications shade handle and drag your finger up the screen. Or, if you find this process frustrating (and it is), touch the Back navigation button at the bottom of the screen.

✔ If you don't deal with notifications, they can stack up!

✔ Notification icons disappear after they've been chosen.

✔ Dismissing certain notifications doesn't prevent them from appearing again in the future. For example, notifications for app updates continue to appear, as do calendar reminders.

✔ Occasionally, status items appear on the notifications shade, such as the USB item from Figure 2-4. These items cannot be dismissed.

✔ Some apps, such as Facebook, don't display notifications unless you're logged in.

✔ The Nexus 7 plays a sound, or *ringtone,* whenever a new notification floats in. You can choose which sound plays; see Chapter 16 for more information.

✔ See Chapter 11 for information on dismissing calendar reminders.

Setting quick actions

When you intend to pull down the notification shade and you fail, you most likely pulled down the Quick Actions instead. That's because, like the notifications shade, the Quick Actions shade also pulls down from the top of the screen. The difference is that you swipe your finger down from the top *right* edge of the screen.

The Quick Actions shade is shown in Figure 2-5. It lists many common settings and options, such as the popular Auto Rotate feature, Airplane Mode, and Wi-Fi. There's also an icon that shows more information about the battery status as well as a button that grants quick access to the Settings app.

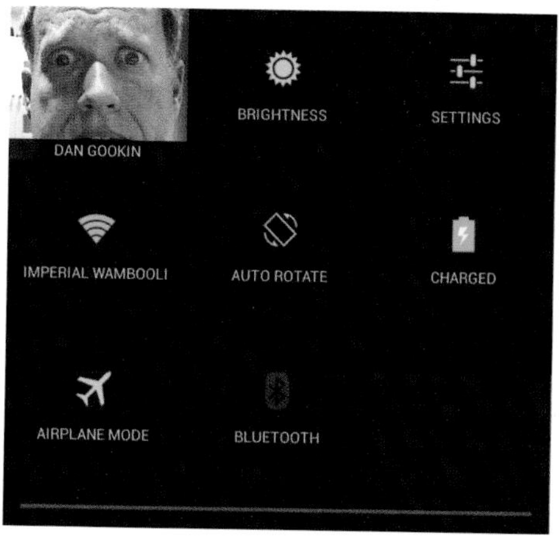

Figure 2-5: The Quick Actions shade.

When you're done viewing the Quick Actions, roll up the shade by flicking your finger or touching the Back button.

✔ Rotation lock is used to disable the tablet's ability to automatically rotate the screen. (Refer to the earlier section "Changing the orientation.") It comes in quite handy, especially when you're using the tablet in a reclined position. Otherwise, the tablet rotates the screen as you jostle around, which can make reading eBooks rather unsettling.

✔ Touch the Settings icon to instantly view the Settings app. This book uses that app quite a bit, so knowing that a shortcut sits atop the notifications shade is handy information.

Visiting the All Apps screen

The application icons you see on the Home screen don't represent all the apps in your Nexus 7. Those icons aren't even applications themselves — they're shortcuts. To see all applications installed on your Nexus 7, you must visit the All Apps screen. To do so, touch the All Apps button on the Home screen. You see the first panel of the All Apps screen, as shown in Figure 2-6.

Apps

Show apps.   Google Play Store

Show widgets.

Swipe to see more apps.

Figure 2-6: The All Apps screen.

You can find any additional apps by swiping the All Apps screen to the left. Continue sliding panels to the left, and you begin to see the widgets available for use on the Home screen. Or you can choose the Widgets category, as illustrated in Figure 2-6.

✔ As you install apps, they're added to the All Apps screen. New apps are inserted alphabetically, which means that any time you add an app, the All Apps screen is re-sorted. That makes it difficult to locate apps by memory, though my advice in Chapter 16 is to place on the Home screen the apps you use most often.

✔ See Chapter 12 for information on getting more apps for your Nexus 7.

Reviewing recent apps

If you're like me, you probably use the same apps over and over on your Nexus 7. You can easily access the list of recent apps by touching the Recent Apps navigation button at the bottom of the Home screen. When you do, you see a pop-up list of the apps you've most recently accessed, similar to the list shown in Figure 2-7.

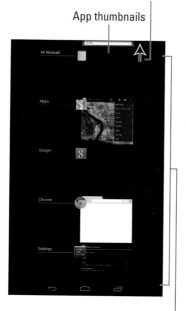

Scroll up for more.

App thumbnails

Recent apps

Figure 2-7: Recently used apps.

To reopen an app, choose it from the list. Otherwise, you can hide the Recently Used Apps list by touching the Back navigation button.

For the programs you use all the time, consider creating shortcuts on the Home screen. Chapter 16 describes how to create shortcuts for apps and all sorts of other fun stuff.

Chapter 3

Text Typing and Editing

*T*he topic is communications. How do you, a human, communicate with the Nexus 7, which is essentially a flat piece of electronics concealed behind a sheet of glass? Unlike communicating with other humans, you can't poke the Nexus 7 with a sharp stick or hit it with a rock to get its attention. Nope, you have to be more clever than that.

Communicating with the Nexus 7 involves the interesting prospect of typing on a touchscreen. A modicum of text editing is required as well, though I doubt that anyone would write a novel on the Nexus 7. Finally, there's the useful dictation feature. The Nexus 7, like some of your fellow humans, understands the words you utter. It's an amazing thing, the details of which are revealed in this chapter.

The Old Hunt-and-Peck

The old mechanical typewriters required a lot of effort to press their keys. It was forceful: clackity-clack-clack. Electronic typewriters made typing easier. And, of course, the computer is *the* easiest thing to type on. A tablet? This device takes some getting used to because its keys are merely flat rectangles on a touchscreen. If this concept doesn't drive you nuts, typing on a tablet is something you should master with relative ease.

Using the onscreen keyboard

When it comes time to create text on the Nexus 7, you see the onscreen keyboard pop into view, right at the bottom of the screen. The onscreen keyboard appears whenever the tablet demands text input or when you have an opportunity to type something.

The basic onscreen keyboard is shown in Figure 3-1. You'll be relieved to see that it's similar to the standard computer keyboard, though some of its keys change their function, depending on what you're typing.

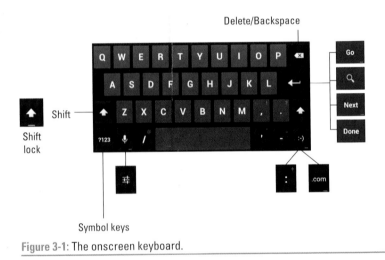

Figure 3-1: The onscreen keyboard.

Figure 3-1 illustrates the onscreen keyboard in Alphabetic mode. You see keys from A through Z. The Shift keys are used for producing capital letters and accessing the symbols that microscopically appear on certain keys, just as on a computer keyboard. You can also use the Delete key, which works to backspace and erase.

The Enter key, below the Delete key, changes its look depending on what you're typing. The variations are shown in Figure 3-1. Here's what each one does:

   Enter/Return: Just like the Enter or Return key on your computer keyboard, this key ends a paragraph of text. It's used mostly when filling in long stretches of text or when multiline input is available.

   Go: This action key directs the app to proceed with a search, accept input, or perform another action.

Search: You see the Search key appear whenever you're searching for something on the tablet. Touching the key starts the search.

Next: This key appears whenever you're typing information into multiple fields. Touching this key switches from one field to the next, such as when typing a username and password.

Done: This key appears whenever you've finished typing text in the final field of a screen that has several fields. Sometimes it dismisses the onscreen keyboard, sometimes not.

The large key at the bottom center of the onscreen keyboard is the Space key. The keys to the left and right of the Space key may change, depending on what type of input is required. For example, the Smiley key turns into the .com key when you type e-mail or web page addresses. The colon key may also appear at that spot.

You use the Microphone key for dictation, which is covered later in this chapter. This key may change to the Settings button, which is used to adjust the onscreen keyboard.

Also see the next section for accessing the number-or-symbol keys on the onscreen keyboard.

✔ If you pine for a real keyboard, one that exists in the fourth dimension, you're not stuck. See the nearby sidebar, "A real keyboard!"

✔ To dismiss the onscreen keyboard, touch the Back navigation button. This button changes its appearance, as shown in the margin, when the onscreen keyboard is visible.

✔ To re-summon the keyboard, touch any text field or spot on the screen where typing is permitted.

✔ To set the Shift Lock (also known as Caps Lock), double-tap either Shift key. A blue bar appears on the Shift key whenever Shift Lock is active.

✔ The Microphone key appears only when dictation is allowed.

✔ Also, the Microphone key may not appear unless you have enabled voice input. See the later section "Activating voice input on the keyboard."

✔ Some keys (such as Microphone, Go, Next, and .com — refer to Figure 3-1) sport three tiny dots. These dots indicate that the key can be pressed to see a pop-up palette of additional characters or options. To see the palette, long-press any key that sports the three dots. You can then drag your finger (don't lift it from the screen) to choose another key or option.

✔ Long-pressing the Microphone key displays the Settings key.

✔ The keyboard reorients itself whenever you turn the tablet to a horizontal position. You may find typing easier in that orientation.

Accessing symbols

You're not limited to typing only the characters you see on the alphabetic keyboard, shown earlier, in Figure 3-1. The onscreen keyboard has many more symbols available, which you can see by touching the ?123 key. Touching this key gives you access to two additional keyboard layouts, as shown in Figure 3-2.

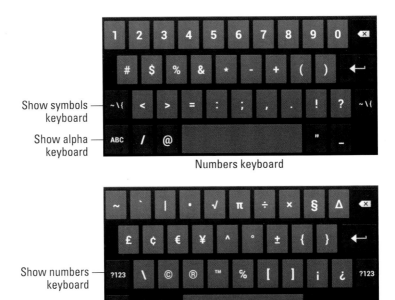

Numbers keyboard

Symbols keyboard

Figure 3-2: The numbers and symbols keyboards.

Touch the ~\{ key to see another symbol-packed keyboard, as illustrated in Figure 3-2.

To return to the standard "alpha" keyboard (refer to Figure 3-1), touch the ABC key.

You can access even more symbols, such as special accented characters, if you know the secret: *Long-press* (touch and hold) a key.

A real keyboard!

If typing is your thing and the onscreen keyboard doesn't do it for you, consider getting a Bluetooth keyboard for your Nexus 7. The Bluetooth keyboard connects wirelessly with your tablet, giving you not only a full-size, full-action keyboard but also all the divine goodness that wireless brings.

The Nexus 7 works with any Bluetooth keyboard, and you can read more about Bluetooth in Chapter 13.

Additional keyboard options may be available for the Nexus 7 in the future. Beyond Bluetooth, keyboard docking stations may be available, or options for connecting a USB keyboard to the tablet — though that kind of flies in the face of the whole wireless paradigm.

When you do, you see a pop-up palette of additional characters, similar to the ones shown for the A key in Figure 3-3.

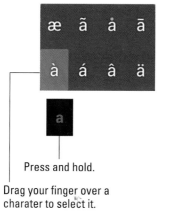

Press and hold.

Drag your finger over a charater to select it.

Figure 3-3: Special symbols palette pop-up thing.

Choose a character by dragging your finger over the palette. Release your finger over the character you want.

Not every character has a special pop-up palette.

Typing duties

It's cinchy to type on the onscreen keyboard: Press a letter to produce the character. It works just like a computer keyboard, though it's flat and there's no action.

As you type, the key you touch is highlighted. You may also hear a clicking sound, which is good for feedback. Typing on a touchscreen is easy to get used to, but I still find that using a physical keyboard is the best way to type.

- ✐ Above all, it helps to *type slowly* until you get used to the keyboard.

- ✐ When you make a mistake, press the Delete key to back up and erase. Press and hold the Delete key to back up faster.

- ✐ A blinking cursor on the touchscreen shows where new text appears, which is similar to how text input works on your computer.

- ✐ When you type a password, the character you type appears briefly, but for security reasons, it's then replaced by a black dot.

    See the later section "Text Editing" for more details on editing your text.

Fixing your text automagically

As a Nexus 7 owner, there's no need to be embarrassed by your typing or inability to spell. That's because the Android keyboard sports two handy features that you'll find most forgiving: Auto Correct and Next Word Prediction.

To see these features in action, start typing something. As you do, word predictions appear just above the keyboard. Here are some things you can do:

- ✐ Tap a word suggestion to instantly type that word. Try to keep up! Sometimes, you can type a whole sentence by simply tapping out suggestions.

- ✐ To select the highlighted word, simply tap the Space key. This trick works only when a highlighted word is in the list.

- ✐ To see further suggestions, long-press a word with three dots beneath it, such as the word *luck*, as shown in Figure 3-4. You see a pop-up palette of suggestions. Drag your finger up, and release it over a specific word to "type" that word.

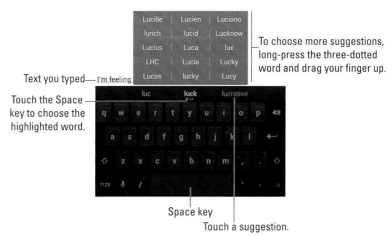

Text you typed— I'm feeling

To choose more suggestions,
long-press the three-dotted
word and drag your finger up.

Touch the Space
key to choose the
highlighted word.

Space key

Touch a suggestion.

Figure 3-4: The Nexus 7 suggests some words.

To ensure that these options are set on your tablet, follow these steps:

1. **Touch the Settings key to summon the Input Options menu.**

   If you don't see the Settings key, long-press the Microphone key, and then drag your finger up to choose the Settings key.

2. **Choose Android Keyboard Settings from the Input Options menu.**

   The Android Keyboard Settings screen appears.

3. **Ensure that a check mark appears by the item Sound on Keypress.**

   Yeah, this isn't the Auto Correction or Next Word Prediction item, but it's nice to set the audio feedback option.

4. **Choose Auto Correction.**

5. **Ensure that the Modest option is chosen.**

   Modest is the setting normally used by the Nexus 7. If you want more and better corrections, choose Aggressive or Very Aggressive.

6. **Ensure that there's a check mark by the item Next Word Suggestions.**

   If not, touch the box to place a check mark there.

7. **Touch the Back navigation button to dismiss the Android Keyboard Settings screen.**

When the keyboard isn't visible, you can get to the Android keyboard Settings screen by opening the Settings app, found on the All Apps screen. Choose the Language & Input item, and then touch the Settings icon next to the Android Keyboard item. Proceed with Step 3.

Text Editing

You'll probably do more text editing on your Nexus 7 than you realize. That includes the basic stuff, such as spiffing up typos and adding a period here or there as well as complex editing involving cut, copy, and paste. The concepts are the same as you find on a computer — but without a keyboard and mouse, the process can be daunting. This section irons out the text-editing wrinkles.

Moving the cursor

The first part of editing text is to move the cursor to the right spot. The *cursor* is that blinking, vertical line where text appears. On most computing devices, you move the cursor by using a pointing device. The Nexus 7 has no pointing device, but you do: your finger.

To move the cursor, simply touch the spot on the text where you want to move the cursor. To help your precision, a cursor tab appears below the text, as shown in the margin. You can move that tab with your finger to move the cursor around in the text.

After you move the cursor, you can continue to type, use the Delete key to back up and erase, or paste in text that you copied from elsewhere. In fact, if text is ready to be pasted, the Paste button appears above the cursor tab. You use this button to paste in text, as described in the later section "Cutting, copying, and pasting."

Selecting text

Selecting text on the Nexus 7 works just like selecting text in a word processor: You mark the start and end of a block. That chunk of text appears highlighted on the screen.

Text selection starts by long-pressing or double-tapping the text. Upon success, you find a single word selected, as shown in Figure 3-5. Further, you see the Text Selection toolbar appear, also illustrated in the figure.

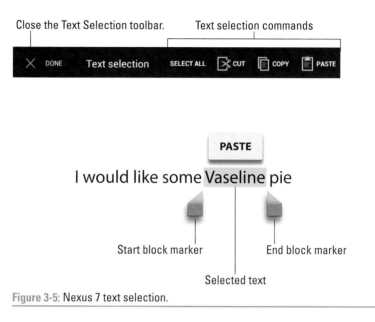

Figure 3-5: Nexus 7 text selection.

Drag the start and end markers around the touchscreen to expand and define the block of selected text. Or you can touch the Select All command at the top of the screen to mark all the text as a single block. (Refer to Figure 3-5.)

After you select the text, you can delete it by touching the Delete key on the onscreen keyboard. You can replace the text by typing something new. Or you can cut or copy the text. See the section "Cutting, copying, and pasting," later in this chapter.

✓ To cancel text selection, just touch anywhere on the touchscreen outside the selected block.

✓ Seeing the onscreen keyboard is a good indication that you can edit and select text. Even so:

Selecting text on a web page

Grabbing a bit of text from a web page works similarly to selecting text elsewhere on your Nexus 7. The difference is that you must long-press the text to start the selection process. (Double-tapping a web page activates the zoom-in feature.) After long-pressing, you can drag the selection markers to mark the block or use the Select All command on the Text Selection toolbar to select all text on the page.

On a web page, the Text Selection toolbar lacks the Cut command but instead supports two other commands: Share and Web Search.

Choose the Share command to send the chunk o' text to another app, send it in an e-mail message, or post it to a social networking site.

Choose the Web Search command to perform a Google search on the selected text.

Touch the Done button on the far left end of the Text Selection toolbar to cancel the web page text selection.

Cutting, copying, and pasting

Selected text is primed for cutting or copying, which works just as it does in your favorite word processor. After you select the text, choose the proper command from the Text Selection toolbar: To copy the text, choose the Copy command. To cut the text, choose Cut.

Just like on your computer, cut or copied text on the Nexus 7 is stored in a clipboard. To paste any previously cut or copied text, move the cursor to the spot where you want the text pasted. The Paste command appears above the cursor tab, as shown earlier, in Figure 3-5, indicating that text can be pasted; touch the Paste button to paste in the text.

> ✔ The Paste command can be anywhere that text is input on the Nexus 7, such as in an e-mail message, a Twitter tweet, or any text field. Odds are good that if you can type, or whenever you see the onscreen keyboard, you can paste text.

> ✔ If you don't see the Paste button above selected text, you can use the Paste command on the Text Selection toolbar.

> ✔ Pasted text replaces any selected text on the screen. If you want to paste in text but not replace text, move the start and end block markers together, and then choose the Paste command from the Text Selection toolbar.

> ✔ The Nexus 7 clipboard can hold only one copied or cut item at a time. As this book goes to press, there's no Clipboard app or method of previewing the item held in the clipboard's storage. That may change in further updates to the tablet's software.

Voice Input

The Nexus 7 has the amazing ability to interpret your utterances and mumblings as text. It works almost as well as computer dictation in science fiction movies, though I can't seem to find the command to destroy the planet Alderaan.

Activating voice input on the keyboard

To ensure that voice input is listening to you and available with the onscreen keyboard, obey these steps:

1. **At the Home screen, touch the All Apps button.**

2. **Open the Settings icon to run the Settings app.**

3. **Choose Language & Input.**

4. **Ensure that there's a check mark in the box by the item Google Voice Typing.**

   If not, touch the box to place a check mark there.

5. **Touch the Home button to return to the Home screen.**

The Microphone button now appears on the onscreen keyboard. See the next section for how to use it.

Dictating to your tablet

Talking to your tablet really works, and works quite well, if you touch the Microphone key on the onscreen keyboard and properly dictate your text.

After touching the Microphone key, you see a special window appear at the bottom of the screen. When the text *Speak Now* appears, dictate your text. Speak directly at the tablet.

As you speak, a Microphone graphic on the screen flashes. The flashing doesn't mean that the Nexus 7 is embarrassed by what you're saying. No, the flashing merely indicates that the tablet is listening, detecting the volume of your voice.

As you blab, the tablet digests what you said, and the text you speak — or a close approximation — appears on the screen. It's magical, though sometimes comical.

✔ The first time you try voice input, you might see a description displayed. Touch the OK button to continue.

✔ The better your diction, the better your results. Also, it helps to speak only a sentence or less.

✔ If you don't like a word that's chosen by the dictation feature, touch it on the screen. You see a pop-up list of alternatives from which you can choose one.

✔ You can edit your voice input just as you edit any text. See the section "Text Editing," earlier in this chapter.

✔ Speak the punctuation in your text. For example, you would say, "I'm sorry comma and it won't happen again" to have the Nexus 7 produce the text I'm sorry, and it won't happen again (or similar wording).

✔ Common punctuation that you can dictate includes the comma, period, exclamation point, question mark, and colon.

✔ Pause your speech before and after speaking punctuation.

✔ There's no way presently to capitalize words you dictate.

✔ Dictation may not work where no Internet connection exists.

Uttering b*** words

The Nexus 7 features a voice censor. It replaces those naughty words you might mumble, placing the word's first letter on the screen, followed by the appropriate number of asterisks.

For example, if *petunia* were a blue word and you uttered *petunia* when dictating text, the Dictation feature would place p****** rather than the word *petunia* on the screen.

Yeah, I know: silly. Or "s****."

The tablet knows a lot of blue terms, including the infamous "Seven Words You Can Never Say on Television," but apparently the terms *crap* and *damn* are fine. Don't ask me how much time I spent researching this topic.

Commanding the Nexus 7 with your voice

You can say "Here, kitty" all you like, but the cat may never come. On the Nexus 7, however, you can use the Voice Search app to find things with your voice and actually meet with some decent results.

Start the Voice Search app by locating it on the All Apps screen. You can also access Voice Search from the Home screen by touching the Microphone icon in the upper-right corner.

After starting the app, you see the Google `Speak now` prompt, along with a glowing microphone icon. Dictate what you want, such as "Restaurants near me." In a few moments, the Nexus 7 runs the proper app and finds what you're looking for.

Examples of what you can utter into the Voice Search app include

Find a good Chinese restaurant

Send e-mail to Obama

Listen to The Monkees

I admit that this feature is a tad unreliable, especially compared with how well voice input works overall. Still, it's worth a try if you truly want to play Mr. Spock and dictate your commands to a cold, impersonal piece of electronics.

Part II
Keep in Touch

The 5th Wave · By Rich Tennant

"That's exactly why I only tweet in my basement."

In this part . . .

These days, it's possible to find yourself physically alone yet be with all your friends. Thanks to the Internet, e-mail, social networking, and forms of instant communications, humanity has become more connected than at any other time in history. Whether that's a miracle or a curse I'll leave up to the (online) philosophers to debate.

Your Nexus 7 is perfectly capable of keeping you connected in the 21st century. You can use your tablet to send and receive e-mail, browse the web, enjoy your online social life, and communicate vocally and visually with friends far and wide. It's one of the many things the Nexus 7 can do, and this part of the book explains how it's done.

Chapter 4

Dealing with Your Friends

. . . .

In This Chapter

▶ Exploring the People app

▶ Searching and sorting your contacts

▶ Adding new contacts

▶ Using the Maps app to add contacts

▶ Editing contacts

▶ Putting a picture on a contact

▶ Deleting contacts

. . . .

*B*ack in the old days, it was important to keep a few important
phone numbers in your head. These days, phone numbers
aren't enough. That's because there's more than one way to
get hold of someone: e-mail, instant messaging, social network
updates, and voice communications over the Internet — plus,
video chat. Trust me: No matter how brilliant you are, you're can't
keep all these various contact points and information tidbits in
your head.

Coming to the rescue is an app on your Nexus 7 called, simply,
People. It's your tablet's address book, your list of contacts. You
can use the People app to organize your friends, send them e-mail,
do social networking (on Google+), and even find them on a map.
But nothing happens with the Nexus 7 and the people you know
until you learn how to deal with your electronic friends. This
chapter explains how it works.

Meet the People

You may already have some friends in your Nexus 7. That's
because your Google account was synchronized with the tablet
when you first set things up. Because all your Gmail and other
types of contacts on the Internet were duplicated on the tablet,

you already have a host of friends available. The place where you can access these folks is the People app.

⌐ If you haven't yet set up a Google account, refer to Chapter 1.

⌐ Adding more contacts is covered later in this chapter, in the section "Even More Friends."

⌐ Most apps on the Nexus 7 use contact information from the People app. These apps include Email and Gmail as well as any app that lets you share information such as photographs or videos.

Using the People app

To peruse the Nexus 7 address book, start the People app: Touch the All Apps button on the Home screen, and then touch the People app icon.

The People app shows a list of all contacts in your Nexus 7, organized alphabetically by first name and similar to the ones shown in Figure 4-1.

Scroll the list by swiping with your finger. Or you can drag the blue thumb button on the left side of the screen to quickly scan the list, as shown in Figure 4-1.

To do anything with a contact, you first have to choose it: Touch a contact name, and you see detailed information on the right side of the screen, as shown in Figure 4-1. The list of activities you can do with the contact depends on the information shown and the apps installed on the tab. Here are some options:

Place a phone call: No, the Nexus 7 isn't a phone, but when you install Skype, touching a contact's phone number activates that app and you can use the tablet to make a call. See Chapter 8 for details.

Send e-mail: Touch the contact's e-mail address to compose an e-mail message using either the Gmail or Email app. When the contact has more than one e-mail address, you can choose to which one you want to send the message. Chapter 5 covers using e-mail on your tablet.

View address: When the contact has a home or business address, you can choose that item to view the address using the Google Earth app or Maps app. When you choose the Maps app, you can then get directions, look at the place using the Street View tool, or do any of a number of interesting things, as covered in Chapter 9.

View Google+ information: Contacts who are in your Google+ circles, or who may be Google+ users, feature the *Connections* heading. You can use the items there to start a conversation, hang out, or add them to a circle, for example. If a contact isn't a Google+ member, you can use the Add Connection button to invite them or start a new connection.

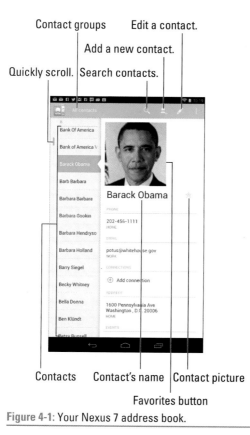

Contact groups   Edit a contact.
Add a new contact.
Quickly scroll. | Search contacts.

Contacts   Contact's name | Contact picture
Favorites button

Figure 4-1: Your Nexus 7 address book.

Some tidbits of information that show up for a contact have no associated action. For example, the tablet doesn't sing *Happy Birthday* when you touch a contact's birthday information.

Sorting your contacts

Your contacts are displayed in the People app in a certain order: alphabetically by first name, first name first. You can change the order, if you like. Here's how:

1. Start the People app.

2. **Touch the Menu icon button.**

3. **Choose Settings.**

   The Display Options screen appears, which shows you the settings for viewing your contacts.

4. **Choose the Sort List By command to specify how contacts are sorted: by first name or last name.**

   The People app is configured to show contacts by first name.

5. **Choose View Contact Names By to specify how the contacts appear in the list: first name first or last name first.**

   The People app shows the contacts listed by first name first.

There's no right or wrong way to display your contacts — only whichever method you're used to.

Even More Friends

Having friends is great. Having more friends is better. Keeping all those friends is best. In the People app, myriad ways are available to add more friends or create new contacts. This section lists a few of the more popular and useful methods.

Building a new contact from scratch

Sometimes, it's necessary to create a contact when you actually meet another human being in the real world or when you finally get around to transferring information into the tablet from your old, paper address book. In either instance, you have information to input, and it starts like this:

1. **Open the People app.**

2. **Touch the Add Contact button.**

   Refer to Figure 4-1 for the button's specific location. If you don't see the button, ensure that All Contacts is chosen from the Contact Groups menu.

3. **If prompted, choose your Google account from the menu.**

   I recommend creating new contacts by using Google because it synchronizes the information with the Internet and any other Android gizmos you may own.

4. Fill in the information on the New Contact screen as best you can.

Fill in the text fields with the information you know, as illustrated in Figure 4-2. Touching a field pops up the onscreen keyboard.

Touch to type.

Save and close.   Touch to add photo.

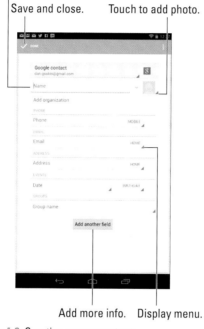

Add more info.   Display menu.

Figure 4-2: Creating a new contact.

Use the Menu button (shown in the margin) to choose options for various items. For example, you can touch the Menu button by the Phone item to select whether the number is a mobile, work, or home number, for example.

To add a second phone number or an e-mail address or a physical address — or any other item — touch the *Add New* text that appears.

To remove an additional item, touch the X button that appears next to the item.

5. Touch the Done button to complete your editing and add the new contact.

Or to cancel the creation of a new contact, touch the Menu button in the upper-right corner of the screen. Choose the Discard command.

New contacts are automatically synced with your Google account. That's one beauty of the Android operating system, used by the Nexus 7: You have no need to duplicate your efforts. Contacts you create on the tablet are instantly updated with your Google account on the Internet.

Creating a contact from an e-mail message

Perhaps one of the easiest ways to build up the Contacts list is to create a new contact from an e-mail message. Follow these steps when you receive a message from someone not already on your Nexus 7 address list:

1. **Touch the Picture button by the contact's name at the top of the message.**

   The Picture button is shown in the margin. If the contact is already in the tablet's address book and they have a picture, the picture shows up. Otherwise, you can use the Menu button in the lower-right corner of the picture icon to summon a menu.

2. **Touch the OK button.**

   If the OK button doesn't show up, the contact is already known to your Nexus 7. You may see a list of information for that contact instead of the prompt to add the contact to the People app.

You can also use this technique to add a new e-mail address for an existing contact. When you do, you're creating a duplicate entry for that person in the People app. See the later section "Joining identical contacts" for information on combining the two address book entries.

Importing contacts from your computer

Your computer's e-mail program is doubtless a useful repository of contacts you've built up over the years. You can export these contacts from your computer's e-mail program and then import them into the Nexus 7. It's not simple, but it's possible.

The key is to save or export your computer e-mail program's records in the *vCard* (.vcf) file format. These records can then be imported by the Nexus 7 into the People app. The method for exporting contacts varies, depending on the e-mail program:

- **In Windows Live Mail:** Choose Go⇨Contacts, and then choose File⇨Export⇨Business Card (.VCF) to export the contacts.

- **In Windows Mail:** Choose File⇨Export⇨Windows Contacts, and then choose vCards (Folder of .VCF Files) from the Export Windows Contacts dialog box. Click the Export button.

- **On the Mac:** Open the Address Book program, and choose File⇨Export⇨Export vCard.

After the vCard files are created on your computer, connect the Nexus 7 to the computer and transfer them. Transferring files from your computer to the Nexus 7 is covered in Chapter 14.

After the vCard files have been copied to the Nexus 7, follow these steps in the People app to complete the process:

1. **Touch the Menu icon button.**

2. **Choose the Import/Export command.**

3. **Choose Import from Storage.**

4. **Select your Google account.**

5. **Choose the option Import All vCard Files.**

6. **Touch the OK button.**

    The contacts are saved on your tablet but are also synchronized to your Gmail account, which instantly creates a backup copy.

The importing process may create duplicates. That's okay: You can join two entries for the same person in the tablet's address book. See the section "Joining identical contacts," later in this chapter.

Beaming contacts

A quick, handy, and extremely high-tech way to send a contact from one device to another is to use the Android Beam feature. To make it happen, both devices must be capable of Near Field Communications, or NFC, and they must sport the Android Beam feature. You already have such a device, the Nexus 7, so your job is to find someone else with a Nexus 7 or an Android Beam–capable gizmo.

To share the contact, open the People app and display the contact's information. Place the back of your tablet (where the NFC field is located) against the other Android Beam device. When the text *Touch to Beam* appears on the screen, tap the screen. The contact information is sent to the other device.

See Chapter 13 for additional information on NFC and Android Beam.

Finding a new contact on the map

When you use the Maps app to locate a coffeehouse, milliner, or hookah parlor, you can quickly create a contact for that location. Here's how:

1. **After searching for your location, touch the cartoon bubble that appears on the map.**

2. **Touch the Menu button.**

3. **Choose Add As a Contact.**

4. **If prompted, choose your Google account as the location under which to create the contact.**

    You see the New Contact screen, with much of the information already filled in. That's because the Maps app shared the info with the People app. It's good when apps play together nicely.

5. **Optionally, add more information, if you know it.**

6. **Touch the Done button.**

    The new contact is created.

See Chapter 9 for detailed information on how to search for a location using the Maps app.

Manage Your Friends

Don't let your friends just sit there, occupying valuable storage space inside the Nexus 7! Put them to work. Or, actually, *you* do the work: Lots of things can be done with your tablet's digital address book. This section lists some routine and common People app activities.

Editing contact information

To make minor touch-ups on any contact, start by locating and displaying the contact's information. Touch the Edit button, shown in the margin, to start making changes.

Change or add information by touching a field and typing on the onscreen keyboard. You can edit information as well: Touch the field to edit and change whatever you want.

If the contact has been joined (so that it's a single entry in the address book but contains information combined from more than one source), you see additional contact information by scrolling down. Sometimes, that information may not be editable.

When you're finished editing, touch the Done button.

Taking a picture of a contact

Nothing can be more delicious than snapping an inappropriate picture of someone you know and using the picture as his contact picture on your Nexus 7. Then, every time he calls you, that embarrassing, potentially career-ending photo comes up.

Oh, and I suppose you could use nice pictures as well, but what's the fun in that?

To use the Nexus 7 to snap a picture of a contact, follow these steps:

1. **Locate and display the contact's information.**
2. **Touch the Edit button.**
3. **Touch the Contact Picture icon button.**
4. **To take a self-portrait, or to hand the Nexus 7 to the contact and have them snap their own picture, choose the command Take Photo.**

   If you're replacing a photo, choose the command Take New Photo.

5. **Use the Nexus 7 like a mirror to snap a picture. Touch the blue Shutter button to take the picture.**

6. Review the picture.

Nothing is set yet. If you want to try again, touch the Refresh button and start over in Step 5.

7. Touch the Check Mark button to confirm the new image.

8. Crop the image as shown in Figure 4-3.

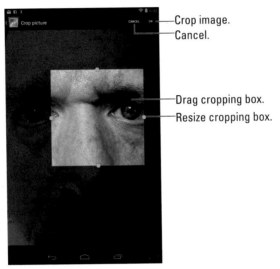

Figure 4-3: Cropping a contact's image.

9. Touch the OK button to crop the image.

The image is cropped but not yet assigned.

10. Touch the Done button to finish editing the contact.

The image is now assigned, and it appears whenever the contact is referenced on your Nexus 7.

This process demonstrates one of the rare times you can use the front-facing camera on your Nexus 7 to snap a picture.

To remove a contact's picture, choose the Remove Photo command in Step 4.

Making a favorite

A *favorite* contact is someone you stay in touch with often. The person doesn't have to be someone you like — only someone you (perhaps unfortunately) contact often, such as your bookie.

Favorite contacts are kept in the Starred group, which can be chosen from the Contact Groups button menu. (Refer to Figure 4-1.)

To add a contact to the Starred group, display the contact's information and touch the Star button by the contact's image, as shown in Figure 4-1. When the star is blue, the contact is one of your favorites and is stored in the Starred group.

To remove a favorite, touch the contact's star again, and it loses its color. Removing a favorite doesn't delete the contact but instead removes it from the Starred group.

By the way, a contact has no idea whether he's one of your favorites, so don't believe that you're hurting his feelings by not making him a favorite.

Joining identical contacts

The Nexus 7 can pull contacts from multiple sources, such as Gmail, Google+, and even other apps such as Skype. You may therefore discover duplicate contact entries in the People app. Rather than fuss over which entry to use, you can join the contacts. Here's how:

1. **Wildly scroll the Contacts list until you locate a duplicate.**

   Well, maybe not *wildly* scroll, but locate a duplicated entry. Because the Contacts list is sorted, the duplicates appear close together (though that may not always be the case).

2. **Select one of the contacts to view it on the right side of the screen.**

3. **Touch the Edit button as though you were editing the duplicate contact.**

4. **Touch the Menu icon button.**

5. **Choose the Join command.**

   The Join Contact(s) window appears. It lists suggested, similar contacts.

   If you see no matching contacts, scroll the list of all contacts to find a match.

6. **Touch a matching contact in the list to join the two contacts.**

   The accounts are merged. Well, they appear together on your Nexus 7.

7. **Touch the Done button to finish editing the contact.**

Joined contacts contain multiple sets of information. You can see the different sets when you edit the contact — each set features its own header that lists the contact's source, such as Google Contact or Google+ Contact.

To split up a contact, edit the entry and choose the Separate command from the Menu icon button. Touch the OK button to burst the single entry into multiple contact entries.

Removing a contact

Every so often, consider reviewing your contacts. Purge the folks whom you no longer recognize, or whom you've forgotten, or the people you flat-out dislike. It's simple:

1. **Display the contact you want to get rid of.**

2. **Touch the Menu icon button.**

3. **Choose Delete.**

4. **Touch OK to remove the contact from your Nexus 7.**

Because the Contacts list is synchronized with your Gmail contacts for your Google account, the contact is also removed there.

Removing a contact doesn't kill the person in real life.

Chapter 5

Messages of the Electronic Kind

*T*he first time an electronic message was sent, it was referred to as *mail*. That's it. Short. Simple. To the point. Eventually, the term *email* was adopted, where the *e* stood for electronic. And that's where the Legion of Editors stepped in. Now you see it written as *E-mail* (which is what my publisher, Wiley, is currently dictating), though *email* is gaining in popularity. There's also *e-mail* (little *E*), *eMail* and even *EMail*. So what is it?

E-mail is this chapter's topic. It's the process of sending a message to someone else, another denizen of the Internet. Using your Nexus 7, you can receive, compose, send, forward, and otherwise review and regard all your e-mail. It's yet another handy way to stay in touch.

Now if the Legion of Editors can only figure out whether *e-mail* or *e-mails* is plural.

Tablet E-Mail

Electronic mail is handled on the Nexus 7 by two apps: Gmail and Email.

The Gmail app hooks directly into your Google Gmail account. In fact, they're exact echoes of each other: The Gmail you receive on your computer is also received on your tablet.

You can also use the Email app to connect with non-Gmail electronic mail, such as the standard mail service provided by your ISP or a web-based e-mail system such as Yahoo! Mail or Windows Live Mail.

Regardless of the app, electronic mail on the Nexus 7 works just as it does on your computer: You can receive mail, create new messages, forward mail, send messages to a group of contacts, and work with attachments, for example. As long as there's a Wi-Fi connection, e-mail works just peachy.

- ✏ Both the Gmail and Email apps are located on the All Apps screen.

- ✏ There's a shortcut to the Gmail app on the Favorites bar at the bottom of the Home screen. It's found in the Google folder at the far left end of the Favorites bar. Adding the Email app icon to the Home screen is easy: See Chapter 16.

- ✏ Although you can use your tablet's web browser to visit the Gmail website, you should use the Gmail app to pick up your Gmail.

- ✏ If you forget your Gmail password, visit this web address:

```
www.google.com/accounts/ForgotPassword
```

Setting up an Email account

The Email app is used to access web-based e-mail, or *webmail,* such as Yahoo!, Windows Live, and what-have-you. It also lets you read e-mail provided by your Internet service provider (ISP), office, or other large, intimidating organization. To get things set up regardless of the service, follow these steps:

1. **Start the Email app.**

   Look for it on the All Apps screen.

   If you haven't yet run the Email app, the first screen you see is Account Setup. Continue with Step 2. Otherwise, you're taken to the Email inbox.

   See the next section for information on adding additional e-mail accounts.

2. Type the e-mail address you use for the account.

There's a .com key on the onscreen keyboard, which you can use to more efficiently type your e-mail address. Look for it in the lower-right corner of the screen.

3. Type the password for that account.

4. Touch the Next button.

If you're lucky, everything is connected smoothly, and you see the Account Options screen. Move on to Step 5.

If you're unlucky, you have to specify the details as provided by your ISP, which include the incoming and outgoing server information, often known by the bewildering acronyms POP3 and SMTP. Plod through the steps on the screen, though you primarily need to specify only the incoming and outgoing server names.

5. Set the account options on the aptly named Account Options screen.

You might want to reset the Inbox Checking Frequency option to something other than 15 minutes.

If the account is to be your main e-mail account, place a green check mark by the option Send Email from this Account by Default.

6. Touch the Next button.

7. Give the account a name and check your own name.

The account is given the name of the mail server, which may not ring a bell with you when it comes to receiving your e-mail. I name my ISP's e-mail account *Main* because it's my main account.

The Your Name field lists your name as it's applied to outgoing messages. So if your name is Joe Yanarapalopadopalous and not jy4457, you can make that change now.

8. Touch the Next button.

You're done.

The next thing you see is your e-mail account inbox. The Nexus 7 synchronizes any pending e-mail you have in your account, updating the inbox immediately. See the later section "You've Got E-Mail" for what to do next.

Adding even more e-mail accounts

The Email app can be configured to pick up mail from multiple sources. If you have a Yahoo! Mail or Windows Live account, or maybe your corporate account, in addition to your ISP's account, you can add them. Follow through with these steps:

1. **Visit the All Apps screen to and start the Settings app.**

2. **Choose Add Account.**

   It's found in the Accounts area, by the big plus sign.

   You see the Add Account menu, which lists a swath of various account types you can add to the Nexus 7.

3. **If your account type is shown in the list, such as Yahoo! Mail, choose it. Otherwise, choose the Email icon.**

   For accessing your evil organization's Microsoft Outlook Exchange server, choose the Corporate option.

4. **Type the account's e-mail address.**

5. **Type the password for the account.**

6. **You can leave empty the box by the option Send Email from This Account by Default.**

   Select this box only when you're adding your primary e-mail account.

7. **Touch the Next button.**

   In a few magical moments, the e-mail account is configured and added to the account list.

   If you goofed up the account name or password, you're warned: Try again. Or if the account requires additional setup, use the information provided by the ISP or another source to help you fill in the appropriate fields.

   Upon success, you see the Account Options screen. Or if you're adding an Exchange Server (a corporate) account, you see the Server Settings screen.

8. **Set any options that thrill you.**

   Most of the preset choices are fine for a web-based, or IMAP, e-mail account. For a corporate account, confirm the settings with your corporate IT Benevolent Dictator. (Though that person will probably just set up the account for you.)

9. **Touch the Next button.**

10. **Name the account.**

     On my tablet, the account was named with my e-mail address. Wrong! I typed in the web-based e-mail service name.

11. **Touch the Next button.**

     The e-mail account has been set up.

You can repeat the steps in this section to add more e-mail accounts. All the accounts you configure are made available through the Email app.

For some corporate accounts, you may be prompted to activate the Device Administrator option. That's a fancy term for allowing your corporate IT humans access to your Nexus 7 remotely to control e-mail. If you're shackled to corporate e-mail, you've probably already agreed to such a thing when you signed up to be an employee. Otherwise, keep in mind that you can always get your corporate e-mail at work, and you may not even need to use your Nexus 7 for that purpose.

You've Got E-Mail

The Nexus 7 works flawlessly with Gmail. In fact, if Gmail is already set up to be your main e-mail address, you'll enjoy having access to your messages all the time by using your tablet.

Non-Gmail e-mail, handled by the Email app, must be set up before it can be used, as covered earlier in this chapter. After completing the quick and occasionally painless setup, you can receive e-mail on your tablet just as you can on a computer.

Getting a new message

You're alerted to the arrival of a new e-mail message in your tablet by a notification icon. The icon differs depending on the e-mail's source.

For a new Gmail message, you see the New Gmail notification, shown in the margin, appear at the top of the touchscreen.

For a new e-mail message, you see the New Email notification.

Pull down the notifications shade to review your e-mail notifications. You see either a single notification representing the most recent message or the total number of pending messages listing the various senders and subjects.

Choosing an e-mail notification takes you to the appropriate e-mail inbox.

Checking the inbox

To peruse your Gmail, start the Gmail app. The Gmail inbox is shown in Figure 5-1.

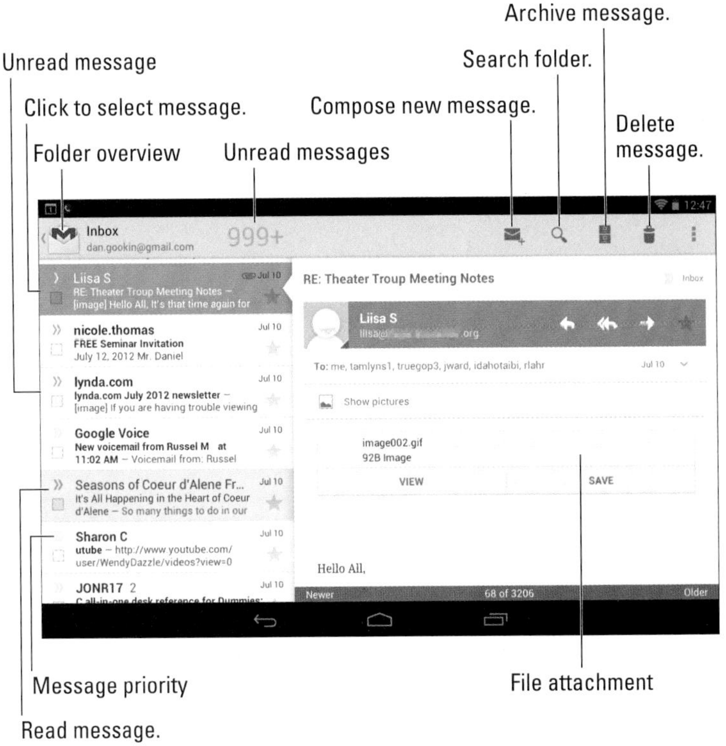

Archive message.

Unread message   Search folder.

Click to select message.   Compose new message.
                                                                        Delete
Folder overview   Unread messages   message.

Message priority   File attachment

Read message.

Figure 5-1: The Gmail inbox.

To check your Email inbox, open the Email app. You're taken to the inbox for your primary e-mail account.

When your multiple e-mail accounts are accessed from the Email app, you can view your universal inbox by choosing the Combined View command from the Account menu, as shown in Figure 5-2.

Figure 5-2: Messages in the Email app.

Don't bother looking for your Gmail inbox in the Combined View window. (Refer to Figure 5-2.) Gmail is its own app; your Gmail messages don't show up in the universal inbox.

↙ See the later section "Setting the primary e-mail account" for information on setting the primary e-mail account.

↙ Search your Gmail messages by pressing the Search button, as shown earlier, in Figure 5-1.

↙ Gmail is organized using *labels,* not folders. To see your Gmail labels from the inbox, touch the Folder Overview button. It's found in the upper-left corner of the screen.

↙ The Email app accesses all your non-Gmail accounts.

↙ Multiple e-mail accounts that are gathered in the Email app are color coded. When you view the combined inbox, you see a color code to the left of each message — if messages from multiple accounts are available.

✓ Scroll the message list in the Email app to view older messages. The Newer and Older buttons move you through the messages one at a time.

Reading an e-mail message

As mail comes in, you can read it by choosing a new e-mail notification, as described earlier in this chapter. Reading and working with the message operate much the same whether you're using the Gmail app or Email app.

Choose a message to read by touching the message on the left side of the screen, as illustrated in Figures 5-1 and 5-2. The message text appears on the right side of the window, which you can scroll up or down by using your finger.

To access additional e-mail commands, touch the Menu button that appears in the upper-right corner of the screen (shown in the margin). The commands that are available on the menu depend on what you're doing in the Gmail app or Email app at the time you touch the button.

✓ Before reading a message, you may have to choose the inbox from the labels or folders on the left side of the screen.

✓ Touch the star by a message to help you more quickly find it in the future. Starred messages can be viewed or searched separately.

✓ If you properly configure the Email program, there's no need to delete messages you read. See the section "Configuring the e-mail delete option," later in this chapter.

✓ I find it easier to delete (and manage) Gmail messages from a computer.

Replying to or forwarding a message

After you read an incoming message, you may choose to reply. This chore, as well as the task of forwarding a message, is handled by the blue bar that appears when you read a Gmail or Email message. (Refer to Figures 5-1 and 5-2.) You can use one of these three icon buttons:

Reply: Touch to reply to a message. A new message window appears (as covered in the next section), but the To field is already filled out. The same subject is also referenced, and the original message text is quoted.

Reply All: Touch to respond to *everyone* who received the original message, including folks on the Cc line. Use this option only when everyone else must get a copy of your reply. Because most people find endless Reply All e-mail threads annoying, use the Reply All option judiciously.

Forward: Touch to copy the message contents to someone else.

After choosing any option — Reply, Reply All, or Forward — your next step is to create the new message, which works as described in the next section.

A Message That You Create

The Gmail and Email apps aren't simply ways to receive electronic mail on your Nexus 7 — they can also be used to spawn new mail. This section describes the various ways to create a new message using your tablet.

Composing a new message

Crafting an e-mail epistle on your tablet works exactly like creating one on your computer. Figure 5-3 shows the basic setup.

Here's how to get started with a new message:

1. **Start an e-mail app — either Gmail or Email.**
2. **Touch the Compose icon button.**
3. **Touch the To field and type the e-mail address.**

Add attachment.

Show Cc/Bcc fields.

Discard message.

Fill in the blanks.   Send message.

Figure 5-3: Writing a new e-mail message.

You can type the first few letters of a contact's name and then choose a matching contact from the list that's displayed.

4. **Type a subject.**

5. **Type the message.**

6. **Touch the Send button to whisk your missive to the Internet for immediate delivery.**

Copies of the messages you send in the Email program are stored in the Sent mailbox. If you're using Gmail, copies are saved in your Gmail account, which you can access from your Nexus 7 or from any computer or mobile device connected to the Internet.

⮞ The Email app features two additional icon buttons, just to the right of the Send button: Save Draft and Discard. To get to the Save Draft and Discard commands in Gmail, you need to touch the Menu button in the upper-right corner of the screen.

⮞ Choose the Save Draft command to store the message in the Drafts folder. You can open that folder to edit the message. Touch Send to send it.

✔ To cancel a message, choose the Discard command from the menu or touch the Trash button, as shown in the margin. Touch the OK button to confirm.

✔ To summon the Cc field in Gmail, press the +Cc/Bcc button, as shown in Figure 5-3. The Cc (Carbon Copy) and Bcc (Blind Carbon Copy) fields appear, eager for you to fill them in.

✔ Refer to Chapter 4 for more information on the Contacts list.

✔ Chapter 3 covers typing, voice input, and text editing.

Sending e-mail to a contact

A quick and easy way to compose a new message is to find a contact and then create a message using that contact's information. Heed these steps:

1. Open the People app.

See Chapter 4 for details.

2. Locate the contact to whom you want to send an electronic message.

Review Chapter 8 for ways to hunt down contacts in a long list.

3. Touch the contact's e-mail address.

4. Choose Gmail to send the message using Gmail, or touch Email to compose an e-mail message using your main e-mail account.

Other options may appear on the Complete Action Using menu. For example, a custom e-mail app you've downloaded may show up there as well.

At this point, creating the message works as described in the preceding section; look there for additional information.

E-Mail Configuration

You can have oodles of fun and waste oceans of time confirming and customizing the e-mail experience on your Nexus 7. The most interesting things you can do are to modify or create an e-mail signature, specify how mail you retrieve on the tablet is deleted from the server, and assign a default e-mail account for the Email app.

Creating a signature

I highly recommend that you create a custom e-mail signature for sending messages from your Nexus 7. Here's my signature:

```
DAN

This was sent from my Nexus 7.
Typos, no matter how hilarious, are unintentional.
```

To create a signature for Gmail, obey these directions:

1. **Start the Gmail app.**
2. **Touch the Menu icon button.**
3. **Choose Settings.**
4. **Choose your Gmail account (your address).**

   Yes, your e-mail address is a command on a menu. It's not just sitting there to be informative.

5. **Choose Signature.**
6. **Type or dictate your signature.**
7. **Touch OK.**

You can obey these same steps to change your signature; the existing signature shows up after Step 5.

To set a signature for the Email app, heed these steps:

1. **In the Email app, touch the Menu icon button.**
2. **Choose Settings.**
3. **Choose an account.**

   The accounts are named after your e-mail address, unless you gave them another name when you first set things up.

4. **Choose Signature.**
5. **Type or dictate your new outgoing e-mail signature.**
6. **Touch the OK button.**

When you have multiple e-mail accounts, repeat these steps to configure a signature for each one.

Configuring the e-mail delete option

 Non-Gmail e-mail that you fetch on your Nexus 7 is typically left on the e-mail server. That's because, unlike your computer's e-mail program, the Email app doesn't delete messages after it picks them up. The advantage is that you can retrieve the same messages later, using your computer. The disadvantage is that you end up retrieving mail you've already read and, possibly, replied to.

You can control whether the Email app removes messages after they're picked up. Follow these steps:

1. **In the Email app, touch the Menu icon button.**

2. **Choose Settings.**

3. **Choose an e-mail account.**

4. **Choose the Incoming Settings command.**

   If there's no Incoming Settings command, you're dealing with a web-based e-mail account, in which case you don't need to need to worry about the manual delete option.

5. **Touch the menu box next to the item Delete Email from Server.**

   It might say *Never* there right now. Anyway, that text is a button, not text.

6. **Choose the option When I Delete from Inbox.**

7. **Touch the Done button.**

   You may need to hide the onscreen keyboard to find the Done button.

When you delete a message in the Email app on your Nexus 7, the message is also deleted from the mail server. It isn't picked up again, not by the tablet, another mobile device, or any computer that fetches e-mail from that same account.

   ✓ Mail that you retrieve using your computer's mail program is deleted from the mail server after it's picked up. That's normal behavior. Your Nexus 7 cannot pick up mail from the server if your computer has already deleted it.

   ✓ Deleting mail on the server isn't a problem for Gmail. No matter how you access your Gmail mail, from your tablet or from a computer, the inbox lists the same messages.

˙Setting the primary e-mail account

When you have more than one e-mail account, the main account — the *default* — is the one used by the Email app to send messages. To change the primary mail account, follow these steps:

1. **Start the Email app.**
2. **Touch the Menu icon button.**
3. **Choose Settings.**
4. **Choose the e-mail account that you want to mark as the primary account.**
5. **On the next screen, place a blue check mark by the Default Account item.**

The messages you compose and send using the Email app are sent from the account you specified in Step 4.

Chapter 6

On the Web

1'm certain that the World Wide Web was designed to be viewed on a computer. The monitor is big and roomy. Web pages are displayed amply, like Uncle Bill on the sofa watching a ballgame. The smaller the screen, however, the more difficult it is to view web pages designed for those roomy monitors. The web on a cell phone? Tragic. But on the Nexus 7?

The Nexus 7 doesn't have the diminutive screen of a cell phone. Nor does it have a huge, cinematic computer monitor. Instead, the tablet's screen is a good size in between. Viewing the web is like seeing a younger, thinner version of Uncle Bill sitting in the Hepplewhite. It's enjoyable, especially when you've read the tips and suggestions in this chapter on surfing the web with your Nexus 7.

Nexus 7 Web Browsing

It's difficult these days to find someone who has no experience with the World Wide Web. More common is someone who has used the web on a computer but has yet to sample the Internet waters on a mobile device. If that's you, consider this section your quick mobile web orientation.

Viewing the web

Your Nexus 7's web browsing app is named Chrome. It's the same web browser found on desktop computers, also known as Google Chrome. Yeah, Chrome is part of the whole googly thing with the Nexus 7.

The Chrome app is found on the Favorites bar on the Home screen, in the far left folder, chock-full of Google apps. Or like all apps on your tablet, it can be found on the All Apps screen. Figure 6-1 illustrates the Chrome app's interface.

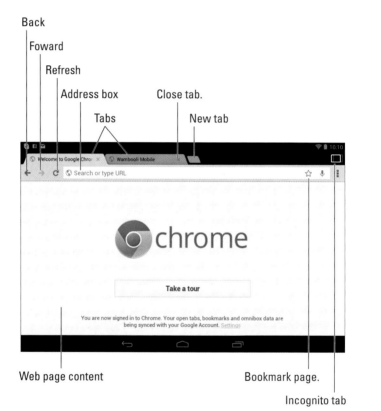

Back

Foward

Refresh

Address box   Close tab.

Tabs   New tab

Web page content   Bookmark page.

Incognito tab

Figure 6-1: The Chrome web browser.

Here are some handy Nexus 7 web browsing tips:

✔ Pan the web page by dragging your finger across the touchscreen. You can pan up, down, left, or right when the page is larger than the tablet's screen.

✏ Pinch the screen to zoom out, or spread two fingers to zoom in.

✏ You can orient the tablet vertically to read a web page in Portrait mode. Doing so may reformat some web pages, which can make long lines of text easier to read.

Visiting a web page

To visit a web page, type its address into the Address box. (Refer to Figure 6-1.) You can also type a search word or phrase if you don't know the exact address of a web page. Touch the Go button on the onscreen keyboard to search the web or visit a specific web page.

You "click" links on a page by touching them with your finger. If you have trouble stabbing the correct link, zoom in on the page and try again.

✏ To reload a web page, touch the Refresh symbol on the left end of the Address bar.

✏ To stop a web page from loading, touch the X that appears to the left of the Address bar. The X replaces the Refresh button and appears only when a web page is loading.

✏ Many websites feature special mobile editions, which automatically appear whenever you visit those sites using a device such as the Nexus 7. If you prefer not to automatically visit the mobile version of a website, touch the Menu button and choose the Request Desktop Site command. When that item is selected, the Chrome app no longer shows the mobile version of a website.

Browsing back and forth

To return to a web page, you can touch the Back button, shown in Figure 6-1, or press the Back navigation button at the bottom of the screen.

Touch the Chrome app's Forward button to go forward or to return to a page you were visiting before you touched the Back button.

Working with bookmarks

Bookmarks are those electronic breadcrumbs you can drop as you wander the web. Need to revisit a website? Just look up its bookmark. This advice assumes, of course, that you bother to create (I prefer *drop*) a bookmark when you first visit the site.

 The cinchy way to bookmark a page is to touch the favorite (star) icon on the right end of the Address bar. Tap that icon, and you see the Add Bookmark window, shown in Figure 6-2.

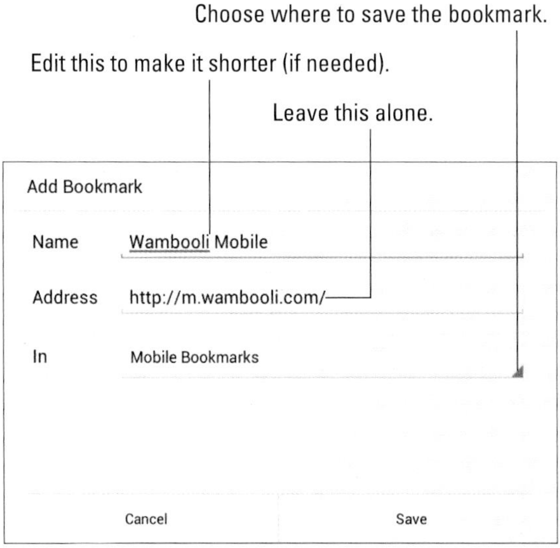

Choose where to save the bookmark.

Edit this to make it shorter (if needed).

Leave this alone.

Add Bookmark

Name   Wambooli Mobile

Address   http://m.wambooli.com/

In   Mobile Bookmarks

Cancel   Save

Figure 6-2: Creating a bookmark.

I typically edit the label to make it shorter, especially if the web page's title is long. Shorter names look better in the Bookmarks window. Touch the Save button, and you've added the bookmark.

After the bookmark is set, it appears in the list of bookmarks. To see the bookmark list, touch the Menu button in the Chrome app's main window, and choose the Bookmarks command. Chrome has three categories for bookmarks: Desktop Bookmarks, Other Bookmarks, and Mobile Bookmarks. (You choose the category from the Add Bookmark window; refer to Figure 6-2.)

The Desktop Bookmarks folder contains any bookmarks you've used on the desktop version of Chrome, which is a handy way to import your computer's bookmarks. That information is coordinated with your Nexus 7, courtesy of your Google account.

To browse bookmarks, open a bookmark folder. If necessary, touch a subfolder to open it. Then touch a bookmark to visit that page.

✔ Remove a bookmark by long-pressing its entry in the Bookmarks list. Choose the command Delete Bookmark. The bookmark is gone.

✔ Bookmarked websites can also be placed on the Home screen: Long-press the bookmark thumbnail, and choose the command Add to Home Screen.

✔ If your desktop Chrome bookmarks aren't coordinated with your Nexus 7, start Chrome on your desktop. Click the settings (wrench) icon and ensure that you're signed in using your Google account.

✔ The MyBookmarks app, available at the Google Play Store, can import your Internet Explorer and Firefox bookmarks from your Windows computer into the Nexus 7. See Chapter 12 for more information on the Google Play Store.

✔ A handy way to create new bookmarks is to review the Most Visited sites in the Chrome app: When perusing your Bookmarks, touch the Most Visited tab at the bottom of the screen. Touch a web page thumbnail to view that page, and then touch the star icon to bookmark that page.

Managing web pages in multiple tabs

The Chrome app uses a tabbed interface to help you access more than one web page at a time. Refer to Figure 6-1 to see various tabs marching across the Chrome app's screen, just above the Address bar.

Here's how you work the tabbed interface:

✔ *To open a blank tab,* touch the teeny tab stub to the right of the last tab, as shown in Figure 6-1.

✔ *To open a link in a new tab,* long-press the link. Choose the command Open in New Tab from the menu that appears.

✔ *To open a bookmark in a new tab,* long-press the bookmark and choose the command Open in New Tab.

You switch between tabs by choosing one from the top of the screen.

Close a tab by touching its Close (X) button. You can close only the tab you're viewing.

✔ The tabs continue marching across the screen, from left to right. You can scroll the tabs to view the ones that have scrolled off the screen.

✔ New tabs open using the home page that's set for the Chrome application. See the later sidebar "Where is the home page?" for information.

✔ If you close all the tabs, you see a blank screen in the Chrome app. The New Tab command appears atop the screen.

✔ New tabs open to the last web page you viewed. Or if you were viewing the bookmarks, the tab opens with the bookmarks. (Bookmarks are web pages, organized internally by the Chrome app.)

✔ For secure browsing, you can open an *incognito tab:* Press the Menu icon button, and choose the command New Incognito Tab. When you go incognito, the Chrome app doesn't track your history or leave cookies or any other evidence of which web pages you've visited on the incognito tab. A short description appears on the incognito tab page, explaining how it works.

✔ To switch between your incognito tabs and regular tabs, touch the rectangle that appears in the upper-right corner of the Chrome app's screen. (Refer to Figure 6-1.)

Searching the web

At the top of every Home screen on your Nexus 7 is the Google Now bar, which is the best way to search the web, the tablet, or just about anything else in your digital life. Touch the bar to summon the Google Now app and begin your search.

✔ See Chapter 11, which covers using Google Now.

✔ You can still visit the Google web page using Chrome on your Nexus 7. Google Now is better.

Searching for something on a web page

To search for something when you're viewing a web page in the Chrome app, follow these steps:

1. **Visit the web page where you want to find a specific tidbit o' text.**

2. **Press the Menu icon button.**

3. **Choose Find in Page.**

4. **Type the text you're searching for.**

5. **Use the up- or down-arrow button to locate that text on the page — up or down, respectively.**

   The found text appears highlighted in yellow.

Touch the Cancel (X) button when you're done searching.

Sharing a page

There it is! That web page you just *have* to talk about to everyone you know. The gauche way to share the page is to copy and paste it. Because you're reading this book, though, you know the better way to share a web page. Heed these steps:

1. **Go to the web page you want to share.**

2. **Touch the Menu icon button and choose the Share command.**

   The Share Via menu appears, listing apps and methods by which you can share the page, as shown in Figure 6-3.

   The variety and number of items on the Share Via menu depend on the apps installed on your tablet. For example, you might see Twitter or Facebook appear, if you've set up those social networking sites as covered in Chapter 7.

Figure 6-3: Options for sharing a web page.

3. Choose a method to share the link.

For example, choose Email to send the link by mail, or Twitter to share the link with your legions of followers.

4. Do whatever happens next.

Whatever happens next depends on how you're sharing the link: Compose the e-mail, create a comment in Facebook, or do whatever. Refer to various chapters in this book for specific directions.

 A handy way to share a web page with your Nexus 7 is to use the NFC feature, commonly known as *Android Beam.* (Not to be confused with Jim Beam.)

To share a web page you're viewing with another Android Beam device, touch your Nexus 7's back to the other device's rear (or wherever NFC is enabled on it). To send the page you're viewing, touch the screen when you see the prompt Touch to Beam.

Similarly, another human with an Android Beam–capable gizmo can send a web page to you: Touch your Nexus 7's back to that other device, and then let the other human touch their screen. The web page is beamed instantly to your tablet, appearing right on the screen.

See Chapter 13 for information on Android Beam.

The Art of Downloading

There's nothing to downloading, other than understanding that most people use the term without knowing exactly what it means. Officially, a *download* is a transfer of information over a network from another source to your gizmo. For your Nexus 7, the network is the Internet, and the other source is a web page.

✓ The Downloading Complete notification appears after the Nexus 7 has downloaded something. You can choose that notification to view the download.

✓ There's no need to download program files to the Nexus 7. If you want new software, you can obtain it from the Google Play Store, covered in Chapter 12.

✓ Most people use the term *download* to refer to copying or transferring a file or other information. The term is technically inaccurate, but the description passes for social discussion.

✔ The opposite of downloading is _uploading,_ the process of sending information from your gizmo to another location on a network.

Grabbing an image from a web page

The simplest thing to download is an image from a web page. It's cinchy: Long-press the image. You see a pop-up menu appear, from which you choose the Save Image command.

To view images you download from the web, you use the Gallery app. Downloaded images are saved in the Download album.

  The image is stored on the tablet's internal storage. It can be found in the /storage/sdcard0/download folder. You can read about Nexus 7 file storage in Chapter 14.

Downloading a file

The web is full of links that don't open in a web browser window. For example, some links automatically download, such as links to PDF files or Microsoft Word documents or other types of files that a web browser is too a-feared to display. Such links are automatically downloaded.

To save other types of links that aren't automatically downloaded, long-press the link and choose the Save Link As command from the menu that appears. If the command doesn't appear, the Nexus 7 cannot save the file, either because the file is of an unrecognized type or because of a security issue.

You view the saved file by using the Downloads app. See the next section.

Reviewing your downloads

The Chrome app keeps a list of all the stuff you download from the web. To review a history of your downloaded stuff, open the Downloads app on the All Apps screen. You see the list of downloads sorted by date, as shown in Figure 6-4.

To view a download, choose it from the list. The Nexus 7 opens the appropriate app to view the download.

  ✔ The Download Manager also lists any web pages you've downloaded.

✔ To remove an item from the Downloads list, place a blue check mark in its box, as shown in Figure 6-4. Touch the trash icon at the top of the screen to remove that download.

✔ Sharing a downloaded item is done by placing a green check mark by the downloaded file and choosing the Share icon button at the top of the screen. (See Figure 6-4.)

✔ You can quickly review any download by choosing the Download notification.

Download history

Download notification.

Delete selected.

Share selected.

Change sort order.

Selected items   Downloads list

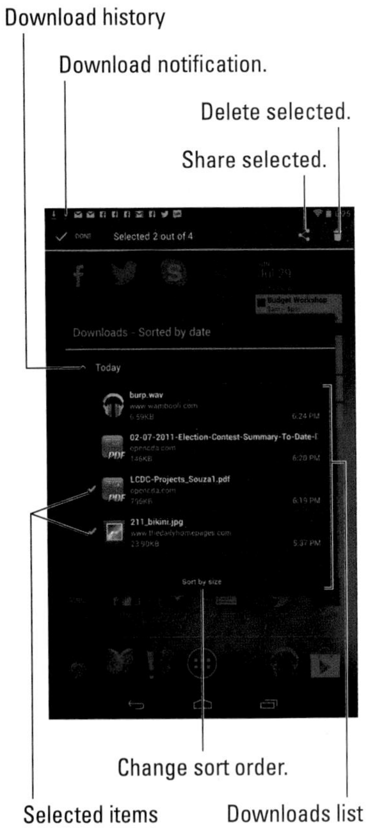

Figure 6-4: The Download Manager.

Chrome Controls and Settings

You could spend all day wandering dreary screens that feature the Chrome app's settings and options. That day can be a special one for you, when you have absolutely nothing else to do. Until then, a couple of settings are worthy of your attention.

Where's the home page?

Unlike any other web browser you've probably ever used, the Chrome app has no *home page*. That page is traditionally the first page you see when you start a web browser. It's also the first page that's loaded when you fire up a new tab. Not so in Chrome.

What you see when you first start Chrome, or add a tab, is often the last web page you visited. If it isn't, you see the Bookmarks screen — specifically, the last bookmark folder you opened. That's the way Chrome works on the Nexus 7.

It's not really terrible that Chrome lacks a home page. To be honest, I pay no attention to the home page on my desktop computer. (My desktop computer uses Chrome, by the way, and it does have a home page.) Normally, in my books on the Android operating system, I offer a tip on how to open a blank home page. That tip is quite popular, so I suppose that not having a home page isn't such a terrible thing.

Changing the way the web looks

You can do a few things to improve the way the web looks on your Nexus 7. First and foremost, don't forget that you can orient the device horizontally or vertically, which rearranges the way a web page is displayed.

From the Settings screen, you can also adjust the zoom setting that's used to display a web page. Heed these steps when using the Chrome app:

1. **Touch the Menu icon button.**
2. **Choose Settings.**
3. **Choose Accessibility.**
4. **Adjust the Text Scaling bar to enlarge or reduce the text size.**

   The scaling bar features a number. A value of 100 percent is normal size (whatever normal is). Higher values make the text larger; smaller values make the text smaller.
5. **Press the Back soft button when you finish setting the Text Scaling value.**

The Preview box, located above the Text Scaling bar, lets you form an idea of how large the text appears on the Nexus 7 screen.

Setting privacy and security options

With regard to security, my advice is always to be smart and think before doing anything questionable on the web. Use common sense. One of the most effective ways that the Bad Guys win is by using *human engineering* to try to trick you into doing something you normally wouldn't do, such as click a link to see a cute animation or a racy picture of a celebrity or politician. As long as you use your noggin, you should be safe.

As far as the Nexus 7's browser settings go, most of the security options are already enabled for you, including the blocking of pop-up windows (which normally spew ads).

If web page cookies concern you, you can clear them from the Settings window. Follow Steps 1 and 2 in the preceding section and choose Privacy. Touch the Clear Browsing Data option, which is found near the upper-right part of the screen.

You can also choose the command Clear Form Data and remove the check mark from Remember Form Data. These two settings prevent any text you've typed into a text field from being summoned automatically by someone who may steal your tablet.

On the main Settings screen, you can choose the Autofill Forms item and adjust the slider to the Off position. Ditto for the Save Passwords setting: Adjust the slider to the Off position. You add security by not saving sensitive information about the websites you visit.

As you use the Nexus 7, you may see various warnings regarding location data. What they mean is that the tablet can take advantage of your location on Planet Earth (using the GPS or satellite position system) to help locate businesses and people near you. I see no security problem in leaving the feature on, though you can disable location services from the Chrome app's Settings screen, on the Content Settings page: Remove the check mark by Enable Location.

Chapter 7

Your Digital Social Life

1 suppose that social networking is the ultimate way to have friends. It's possible to have hundreds and hundreds of friends, and to know what everyone is up to, but never actually meet them face-to-face. What a swell invention! Think of the money mankind can save on deodorant and breath mints!

Equipped with the Nexus 7, you too can foray into the exciting, self-centered world of online social networking. Yeah, I'm not really a big fan of the whole online popularity contest thing. Still, it's a great way to stay in touch and follow family events. This chapter covers options for sharing all your intimate private moments with the entire planet.

Google Wants You to Use Google+

When it comes to social networking, the first thing people think of is Facebook. You can't avoid it. Then maybe someone will mention Twitter. What irks Google is that no one really takes its own social networking site, Google+, seriously. Because you have the Nexus 7, which is a Google tablet, you're given the Google+ app preinstalled to help you begin your social networking journey. No other social networking apps are preinstalled, so the message is clear.

I'm not a big Google+ user, but it does have a spread of features that you may find handy on your Nexus 7. Because of that, I'm obliged to write about it — briefly — in this section. You can also find Google+ information in Chapter 8, which covers its video chat features.

Setting up Google+

Even though you already have a Google account (which you need in order to operate the Nexus 7), you still have to endure the pain of setting up and configuring Google+ on your tablet. The operation works like this:

1. **Start the Google+ app.**

   You find it on the All Apps screen, though a shortcut dwells in the Google folder on the far right end of the Favorites bar.

2. **Choose your Google account from the list.**

   You see your main Gmail account listed. Choose that one.

3. **Type your profile information.**

   Some of it's already filled in, such as your first and last names. If you signed up for Gmail as Harold and you want to be known on Google+ as Harry, you can make that change now.

   You can also choose your gender. I've studied lots of foreign languages, but I'm utterly unfamiliar with the Other gender.

   There's a check mark item for Google ad content. Do you want to be blasted by advertising based on your social networking habits? Think hard.

4. **Touch the Continue button.**

   A list of potential Google+ friends appears, culled from your Gmail Contacts list. Touch the Add circle to make someone your Google+ friend. (Do they call them "friends" in Google+? See? I'm such a Facebook person.)

5. **Touch the Next button until you see the Turn On Instant Upload screen.**

   This item is one that I would normally caution you on: Do you want the Nexus 7 to automatically upload all your photos and videos to Google+? Because the Nexus 7 lacks a rear camera, it probably doesn't matter. But still, consider selecting the Turn Off Instant Upload option to avoid having any of your self-mug–shots unintentionally appearing online.

6. Touch the Done button.

Setup is complete.

You next see the main Google+ screen, which (amazingly) shows lots of information, news items, and updates even when you've never used Google+.

 Don't worry if you want to change your mind on a few of the settings that are made during setup. You can review options by touching the Menu icon button while viewing the Stream. Choose the Settings command. The Instant Upload option can be turned on or off from the screen that appears.

Using Google+

Google+ appears on your tablet, similar to the way it's shown in Figure 7-1. Touch the App button in the upper-left corner of the screen to see the Google+ navigation bar. The Stream (top item) is the main place to go for news updates and such.

Refresh screen.   App button

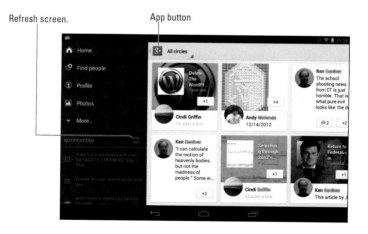

Figure 7-1: Google+.

To compose text messages to your Google+ associates, touch the green pencil icon that appears when viewing your circles. (It's not shown in Figure 7-1, but it appears on the right edge of the screen.) Also see Chapter 8, which covers using the Google Talk app on your tablet.

For video chat, use the Hangout item on the navigation bar. See Chapter 8 for details.

To quit Google+, touch the Home navigation button.

✔ Unlike the other social networking apps covered in this chapter, Google+ is directly tied in with the People app. You can add contacts in the People app to your Google+ circles. See Chapter 4.

✔ The Messenger app, found on the All Apps screen, is basically a shortcut to the Messenger part of Google+. Messenger allows you to text-chat with other Google+ users.

Your Life on Facebook

Of all the social networking sites, Facebook is the king. It's the online place to go to catch up with friends, send messages, express your thoughts, share pictures and videos, play games, and waste more time than you ever thought you had.

✔ Though you can access Facebook on the web by using the Chrome app, I highly recommend that you use the Facebook app described in this section.

✔ Don't look for it: Your Nexus 7 doesn't ship with the Facebook app, but you can easily obtain it, as described later in this section.

✔ Future software updates to the Nexus 7 may include a Facebook app or another social networking app. If so, you can read an update on my website:

```
www.wambooli.com/help/tablets/nexus7/
```

Setting up your Facebook account

The best way to use Facebook is to have a Facebook account, and the best way to do that is to sign up at www.facebook.com by using your computer. Register for a new account by setting up your username and password.

Do not forget your Facebook username and password!

Eventually, the Facebook robots send you a confirmation e-mail. You reply to the message, and the online social networking community braces itself for your long-awaited arrival.

After you're all set up, you're ready to access Facebook on your Nexus 7. To get the most from Facebook, you need a Facebook app. Continue reading in the next section.

Getting the Facebook app

The Nexus 7 doesn't come with a Facebook app, but you can get the Facebook app for free from the Google Play Store. The app is your red carpet to the Facebook social networking kingdom.

The official name of the app is Facebook for Android. It's produced by the Facebook organization itself. You can search for and install this app from the Google Play Store. See Chapter 12.

Running Facebook on your Nexus 7

The first time you behold the Facebook app, you'll probably be asked to sign in. Do so: Type the e-mail address you used to sign up for Facebook, and then type your Facebook password. Touch the Log In button or the Done button on the onscreen keyboard.

Eventually, you see the Facebook News Feed, similar to the one shown in Figure 7-2.

When you're done using Facebook, touch the Home icon button to return to the Home screen.

The Facebook app continues to run until you either sign out or turn off the Nexus 7. To sign out of Facebook, touch the Menu icon button (in the lower-right area of the screen), and choose the Logout command.

Figure 7-2: Facebook on the Nexus 7.

  ✔ Refer to Chapter 16 for information on placing a Facebook app shortcut on the Home screen.

  ✔ Also see Chapter 16 for information on adding the Facebook widget to the Home screen. The Facebook widget displays recent status updates and allows you to share your thoughts directly from the Home screen.

  ✔ The News Feed can be updated by swiping down on the screen.

  ✔ Notifications for Facebook appear at the top of the screen, as shown in the margin as well as in Figure 7-2.

Setting your status

The primary thing you live for on Facebook, besides having more friends than anyone else, is to update your status. It's the best way to share your thoughts with the universe, far cheaper than skywriting and far less offensive than a robocall.

To set your status on the Nexus 7, follow these steps in the
Facebook app:

1. Touch the Status button at the top of the screen.

You see the Update Status screen, where you can type your
musing, similar to the one shown in Figure 7-3.

Status update text

Share status.

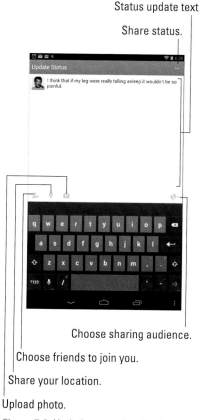

Choose sharing audience.

Choose friends to join you.

Share your location.

Upload photo.

Figure 7-3: Updating your Facebook status.

**2. Type something pithy, newsworthy, or typical of the stuff
you read in Facebook.**

3. Touch the Post button.

You can also set your status by using the Facebook widget on the
home page, if it's been installed: Touch the What's on Your Mind
text box, type your important news tidbit, and touch the Share
button.

Uploading a picture to Facebook

One popular thing to do on Facebook is upload pictures of events and places. It's something that the Facebook app can do, but not completely because the Nexus 7 lacks a rear-facing camera. And having a front-facing camera makes no difference, either: If you attempt to take a picture of yourself using the Facebook app, you're informed that your tablet (or "phone") lacks a camera.

The lack-of-camera issue may be resolved in future updates to the Facebook for Android app or to the Nexus 7 itself. Until then, you can upload pictures from the tablet's digital photo album to Facebook. It works like this:

1. **Touch the Photo button.**

   Refer to Figure 7-2 for its location, or you can use the Upload Photo button found on the status update screen, shown earlier, in Figure 7-3.

2. **Choose an image from the gallery.**

   The Gallery app starts, from which you can browse for and choose a picture to upload.

3. **Tap the image to (optionally) add a tag.**

   You can touch someone's face in the picture and then type their name. Choose from a list of your Facebook friends to apply a name tag to the image.

4. **Touch the Compose button to add a message to the image.**

    The compose button is shown in the margin. At this point, posting the image works just like adding a status update.

5. **Type some text to accompany the image.**

6. **Touch the Post button.**

   The image is posted as soon as it's transferred over the Internet and digested by Facebook.

The image can be found as part of your status update or News Feed, but it's also saved to Facebook's Mobile Uploads album.

✔ Not every image stored in the Gallery can be uploaded to Facebook. Shared Picasa albums, for example, cannot be chosen for uploading to Facebook. You see the message `No permission to access media` if you make the attempt.

✔ Facebook also appears on the various Share menus you find on the Nexus 7. Choose Facebook from the Share menu to send to Facebook whatever it is you're looking at. (Other chapters in this book give you more information about the various Share menus and where they appear.)

Configuring the Facebook app

The commands that control Facebook are stored on the Settings screen, which you access while viewing the main Facebook screen: Touch the Menu icon button, and choose the Settings command.

Choose Refresh Interval to specify how often the Nexus 7 checks for Facebook updates. You might find the one-hour value to be too long for your active Facebook social life, so choose something quicker. Or, to disable Facebook notifications, choose Never.

The following two options determine how the Nexus 7 reacts to Facebook updates:

Vibrate: Vibrates the tablet

Notification Ringtone: Plays a specific ringtone

For the notification ringtone, choose the Silent option when you want the tablet not to make noise upon encountering a Facebook update.

Touch the Back navigation button to close the Settings screen and return to the main Facebook screen.

The Tweet Life

Twitter is a social networking site, similar to Facebook but far briefer. On Twitter, you write short spurts of text that express your thoughts or observations, or you share links. Or you can use Twitter to follow the thoughts and twitterings, or tweets, of other people.

- A message posted on Twitter is a *tweet.*

- A tweet can be no more than 140 characters long. That number includes spaces and punctuation.

- You can post messages on Twitter and follow others who post messages.

- They say that of all the people who have accounts on Twitter, only a small portion of them actively use the service.

- I'm not a big fan of Twitter. It has some good news feeds and local information, but not a lot of it interests me.

Setting up Twitter

The best way to use Twitter on the Nexus 7 is to already have a Twitter account. Start by going to `http://twitter.com` on a computer and following the directions there for creating a new account.

After you've established a Twitter account, obtain the Twitter app for your Nexus 7. The app can be obtained from the Google Play Store. Get the Twitter app from Twitter, Inc. (The Google Play Store features lots of Twitter apps, or *clients.*) Refer to Chapter 12 for additional information on downloading apps to your Nexus 7.

When you start the Twitter app for the first time, touch the Sign In button. Type your Twitter username or e-mail address, and then type your Twitter password. After that, you can use Twitter without having to log in again — until you turn off the tablet or exit the Twitter app.

Figure 7-4 shows the Twitter app's main screen, which shows the current tweet feed.

New tweet notification   Create new tweet.

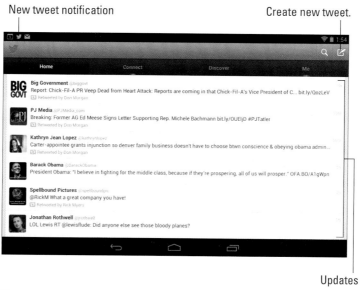

Updates

Figure 7-4: The Twitter app.

See the next section for information on *tweeting,* or updating your
status using the Twitter app.

Tweeting

The Twitter app provides an excellent interface to the many
wonderful and interesting things that Twitter does. Of course, the
two most basic tasks are reading and writing tweets.

To read tweets, choose the Home category, as shown in Figure 7-4,
to view the timeline. Recent tweets are displayed in a list, with the
most recent information at the top. Scroll the list by swiping it with
your finger.

To tweet, touch the new-tweet icon. (Refer to Figure 7-4.) Use the
New Tweet screen, shown in Figure 7-5, to compose your tweet.

I should have typed something
brilliant here before I took the screen shot.

Share the tweet.

Number of characters remaining

Take a picture.   Mention someone.

Share a picture.   Share your location.

Figure 7-5: Creating a tweet.

Touch the Tweet button to share your thoughts with the twitterverse.

✓ You have only 140 characters for creating your tweet. That includes spaces.

✓ The character counter in the Twitter app lets you know how close you are to reaching to the 140-character limit.

✔ Twitter itself doesn't display pictures, other than your account picture. When you send a picture to Twitter, you use an image hosting service and then share the link, or URL, to the image. All this complexity is handled by the Twitter app.

✔ Unlike the Facebook app, the Twitter app can use the Nexus 7's front-facing camera to snap a picture. Use the Take a Picture button (refer to Figure 7-5) to take a self-portrait.

✔ The Twitter app appears on various Share menus in other apps on your Nexus 7. You use these Share menus to send to Twitter whatever you're looking at.

Even More Social Networking

The Internet is brimming with social networking opportunities. Facebook may be the king, but lots of landed gentry are eager for the crown. It almost seems as though a new social networking site pops up every week. Beyond Facebook and Twitter, other social networking sites include, but are not limited to:

✔ LinkedIn

✔ Meebo

✔ Myspace

I recommend first setting up the social networking account on your computer, similar to the way I describe it earlier in this chapter for Facebook and Twitter. After that, obtain an app for the social networking site using the Google Play Store. Set up and configure the app on your Nexus 7 to connect with your existing account.

✔ See Chapter 12 for more information about the Google Play Store.

✔ As with Facebook and Twitter, you may find your social networking apps appearing on various Share menus on the Nexus 7. That way, you can easily share your pictures and other types of media with your online social networking pals.

Chapter 8

Text Chat, Video Chat, and Phone Calls

*N*ot news: The Nexus 7 is not a phone. News: The Nexus 7 can be used to place phone calls. Heck, it even does *video* phone calls. The secret is to know which apps to use. These apps convert your tablet — and its front-facing camera — into the same communications device they promised in the 21st century: the picture phone.

We Can Talk

One of the ways that you can fool your Nexus 7 into acting more like a phone is to use the app called Google Talk. It does text chat, voice chat, and video chat. The only downside to the app is that you can communicate only with your Google contacts. Still, that's good enough for me!

If I were to guess, I would guess that Google Talk may eventually be replaced by the Messenger feature of Google+. They're similar.

Using Google Talk

Get started with Google Talk by starting the Talk app on your Nexus 7. Like all apps, it's located on the All Apps screen, though you can find the Talk app shortcut in the Google folder on the far left side of the Favorites bar.

When you start the Talk app the first time, you're prompted to sign in using your Google account: Touch the Sign In button. Follow the directions on the screen to complete the painful setup.

After signing in, you see the main Talk screen, shown in Figure 8-1. Your Google contacts who have activated Google Talk, on either their computer or a mobile gizmo such as the Nexus 7, appear in a list on the screen. Their *status* (whether they're available to talk) appears by their name. Green dots mean that they're ready to talk. As a bonus, if a video camera is available, you can video-chat.

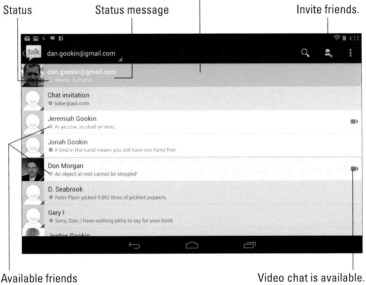

Touch here to set your status.

Status   Status message   Invite friends.

Available friends   Video chat is available.

Figure 8-1: Google Talk.

To sign out of Google Talk, touch the Menu icon button in the upper-right corner of the screen. Choose the Sign Out command.

Setting your status and message

Two items are associated with your account in the Talk app, found on the Friends list as well: your status and the status message.

The *status* tells other Google Talk users whether you're available for a conversation. The *status message* is a bit of text that appears below your name when you're online. Setting either option is done the same way: Touch your account name at the top of the Friends list.

To set your status, touch your account picture, then touch the green bar that lists your current status. Choose one of the options: Available, Busy, or Invisible. There's also a Sign Out option, which sets your status to Offline. If you're available, the status appears as a green dot, as shown in Figure 8-1. A friend who isn't logged in sports a gray X.

To set your status message, touch the status message and type a new one. If I'm not always available to chat, I write, "Give it a try. I may answer."

When you're done setting your status or status message, touch the Back navigation button to return to the main Talk screen.

Getting friends on Google Talk

Yeah, it happens: You don't have any friends. Well, at least you don't have any friends showing up in the Friends list in Google Talk. You can easily fix the problem: Touch the Invite Friends button, as shown in Figure 8-1. Type the friend's e-mail address, and touch the Send Invitations button to send that person an invite.

You receive a reply to your invitation on a mobile device that's running the Talk app or on a computer with the Gmail web page open. When you receive the invitation, you find it listed in the Friends list. Invitations have the heading Chat Invitation.

To accept an incoming invitation, touch the Chat Invitation item in your Friends list. You see the Accept Invitation window. Touch the Accept button to confirm your friendship and, eventually, chat with that person.

Spam robots are out there to entice you to chat. If you don't know the person or don't recognize the e-mail address, don't accept the invitation. Touch the Decline button to politely dismiss the request. If you're certain that the person is a spambot, touch the Block button.

Your friends can be on a computer or mobile device to use Google Talk; it doesn't matter which. But they must have a camera available to enable video chat.

Typing at your friends

The most basic form of communication in the Talk app is *text-chatting*. This term refers to typing at another person, which is probably one of the oldest forms of communications on the Internet. It's also the most tedious, so I'll be brief.

You start text-chatting by touching a contact in the Friends list. Type your message, as shown in Figure 8-2. Touch the Send button to send your comment.

App button   Voice chat

Current chat friend   Conversation   Video chat

Jeremiah Gookin	
On mobile device	

I found $100 on the street today

Very cool. So it was just sitting there?

yes, right next to a dead guy

Uh...I don't think you should keep it.

Type message

Send message.

Figure 8-2: Text-chatting.

You type, your friend types, and so on until you grow tired or the tablet runs out of battery juice.

At any time, you can touch the App button to return to the main screen (your Friends list), as illustrated in Figure 8-2. Then you can simply choose another friend from the list and chat with him.

Resume any conversation by choosing that same contact from the Friends list.

To end a chat, touch the Menu icon button and choose the End Chat command.

Chatting with multiple people is possible: During a chat, touch the Menu icon button, and choose the Add to Chat command. Touch a friend (only available friends are listed) to invite them in.

Talking and video chat

Take the conversation up a notch by touching the Voice button or Video button on the right side of the text-chat window. (Refer to Figure 8-2.) When you do, your friend receives a pop-up invite and Talk notification. Or if a friend is asking you to voice- or video-chat, you see the pop-up. Touch the Accept button to begin talking.

Figure 8-3 shows a video chat. The person you're talking with appears in the big window; you're in the smaller window. With the connection made and the invite accepted, you can begin enjoying video chat.

The onscreen controls (in the upper-right corner of Figure 8-3) may vanish after a second; touch the screen to see the controls again.

To end the conversation, touch the Close (X) button. Well, say "Goodbye" first, and then touch the X button.

  ✔ When you're nude or you just don't want to video-chat, touch the Decline button for the video chat invite. Then choose that contact and reply with a text message or voice chat instead.

  ✔ The X button to end the chat doesn't disappear like the other commands shown in Figure 8-3.

  ✔ Use the Speaker menu to choose how to listen when you video-chat. You can choose to use the tablet's speaker, headphones, and so on.

- The Effects menu has some interesting features available. I find that the Silly Faces option creeps people out the most.

- To exit the Effects menu, touch the App button.

- Touching the smaller of the two preview windows swaps that window's content with the larger window.

- The Nexus 7's front-facing camera is at the top center when the tablet is held vertically. If you want to make eye contact, look directly into the camera, though when you do, you can't see the other person.

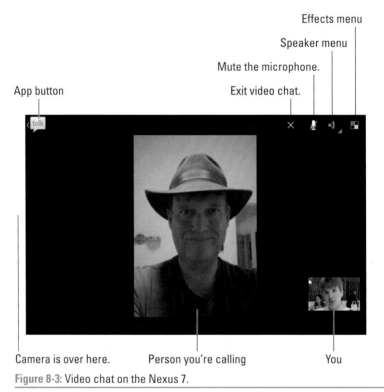

Effects menu

Speaker menu

Mute the microphone.

App button   Exit video chat.

Camera is over here.   Person you're calling   You

Figure 8-3: Video chat on the Nexus 7.

Google+ Hangouts

Video chat with Google Talk involves only you and one other person. Video chat with Google+ can involve a legion of your friends. Well, maybe not that many, but more than two. Your friends have to use Google+ and be available online with a gizmo that sports a front-facing camera. All they have to do after that is start or join a hangout.

To start a hangout, open the Google+ app and obey these steps:

1. Choose Hangouts from the App button menu.

If you don't see the Hangouts item, touch the More button.

The Hangouts screen appears, as illustrated in Figure 8-4. Its purpose is to offer you a chance to invite, or alert, online friends about your hangout and potentially have them join you.

Suggestions

Add contacts from Google+ circles.

Invite list

Start hanging out.

Figure 8-4: Inviting people to your hangout.

2. Invite people to your hangout.

The text box is your invite list, like the To field in an e-mail message. You can type a name, use the Plus (+) button, or pluck a picture on the screen to add them to the invite list. The process is similar to creating a list of contacts for sending an e-mail message.

If you touch the Plus button, the Add People screen appears, where you can fetch contacts from your Google+

circles. Place check marks by your circles or by individuals you want to invite, and then touch the OK button.

The People You May Know list suggests some friends you can quickly invite by touching their contact icons. When you touch an icon, a green check mark appears, and that person's name is added to the invite list.

3. **Start the hangout by touching the Start button.**

   The Start button doesn't work until you've invited at least one other person to the hangout.

4. **Wait.**

   Your invitations fly out to the people you invited. The tablet may ring, like you're listening to an outgoing phone call. Eventually, someone will join and you can video-chat. Others you've invited may join after that.

   If no one joins, you see a disappointing reminder on the screen that you have no friends who want to hang out — or something like that.

5. **Blah. Blah. Blah.**

   Do whatever you would normally do with your friends — talk, make faces, dish about your enemies. It's like being there in person, but you're using the Nexus 7.

   You can add people to the hangout by using the Add button that appears in the upper-right corner of the screen. The Add button appears only when you are the hangout host.

6. **When you're done, end the hangout by touching the red Close (X) button.**

   Because you're the host of the hangout, when you leave, everyone else is tossed out as well. I recommend saying goodbye first.

As a Google+ citizen, you may someday receive an invite from someone you know (or maybe someone you don't know) to join a hangout. When you do, you see either a notification appear atop the screen or, if you're using the Google+ app at the time, an Incoming Hangout screen. To join the hangout, swipe the Camera icon button (shown in the margin) to the right. Your tablet's camera turns on, and you can see the other person (or people) in the hangout. To leave the hangout, touch the red X.

You can mute the speaker or disable video by touching the microphone and camera icons at the bottom of the screen during a hangout.

Connect to the World with Skype

When it comes time to turn your Nexus 7 into a phone, you need something called *Skype.* It's one of the most popular Internet communications programs, allowing you to text-, voice-, or video-chat with others on the Internet as well as use the Internet to make real, honest-to-goodness phone calls.

Getting Skype for the Nexus 7

Your Nexus 7 doesn't come with Skype software preinstalled. To get Skype, saunter on over to the Google Play Store and download the Skype app. In case you find multiple apps, get the one that's from the Skype company itself.

To use Skype, you need a Skype account. You can sign up for one using the app, or you can visit `www.skype.com` on a computer to complete the process.

When you start the Skype app for the first time, work through the start-up screens. You can even take the tour. Be sure to have Skype scour the Nexus 7's address book (the People app) for contacts you can Skype. This process may take a while, but if you're just starting out, it's a great help.

> ✔ Skype is free to use. Text chat is free. Voice and video chat with other Skype users is also free. But if you want to call a real phone, you need to boost your account with Skype Credit.

> ✔ Don't worry about getting a Skype Number, which costs extra. Only if you expect to receive calls using Skype is it necessary.

Chatting with another Skype user

Text chat with Skype works similarly to texting on a cell phone. The only difference is that the other person must be a Skype user. So in that respect, Skype text chat works a lot like Google Talk, covered elsewhere in this chapter.

To chat, follow these steps:

1. **At the main Skype screen, touch the Contacts button.**
2. **Choose a contact.**

3. Type your text in the text box.

The box is found at the bottom of the screen. It says *Type Instant Message Here.*

4. Touch the Return key on the onscreen keyboard to send the message.

As long as your Skype friend is online and eager, you'll be chatting in no time.

At the far right end of the text box, you find the Smiley button. You can use this button to insert a cute graphic into your text.

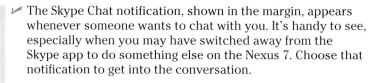

- ✔ The Skype Chat notification, shown in the margin, appears whenever someone wants to chat with you. It's handy to see, especially when you may have switched away from the Skype app to do something else on the Nexus 7. Choose that notification to get into the conversation.

- ✔ You can add more people to the conversation, if you like: Touch the Add (plus) button and choose the command Add (People). Select the contacts you want to join with your chat session, and then touch the Add Selected button. It's a gang chat!

- ✔ To stop chatting, touch the Back navigation button. The conversation is kept in the Skype app, even after the other person has disconnected.

- ✔ For the chat to work, the other user must be online and available.

Seeing on Skype (video call)

Placing a video call with Skype on your Nexus 7 is easy: After choosing a contact — one that's not only available but also has the ability to do video chat — touch the Video Call icon from the top of the contact's information page. The call rings through to the contact, and if they're available, they pick up in no time and you're talking and looking at each other.

Sending a text message with Skype

It's cool that you can use Skype to send a text message. It's simple: Choose a contact who has a real phone number listed as part of their contact information. Choose the SMS item from the contact's information screen. You can then type a text message to them just as though you were using a real phone and not a tablet.

Lamentably, you'll find a few downsides with text messaging on Skype.

The first drawback is that the person to whom you're sending the message probably won't recognize the incoming phone number. My advice is to identify yourself in the message.

The second drawback is that the person may not be able to text you back. They can try, but you have no guarantee of receiving the reply.

The third drawback is that text messaging costs you Skype Credit. As this book goes to press, the fee is a hair over 11 cents per message.

✔ To get Skype Credit, touch the Profile icon on the main Skype screen. Touch the Skype Credit item, and follow the directions onscreen to buy more credit.

✔ *SMS* stands for Short Message Service. Most people just say "text message."

Placing a Skype phone call

Ah. The big enchilada: Skype can be used to turn the Nexus 7 into a cell phone. It's an amazing feat. And it works quite well. Heed these steps:

1. **Ensure that you have Skype Credit.**

   You can't make a "real" phone call unless you have Skype Credit on your account. You add Skype Credit by touching the Profile button on the main Skype screen and choosing Skype Credit.

2. **Choose a contact to call.**

   Your Skype contact must have a phone number listed in their information. Otherwise you'll have to dial the number directly, which is described near the end of this section.

3. **Touch the Phone icon in the upper-right corner of the screen.**

4. Talk.

The In-Call screen looks similar to the one in Figure 8-5.

Skype contact info

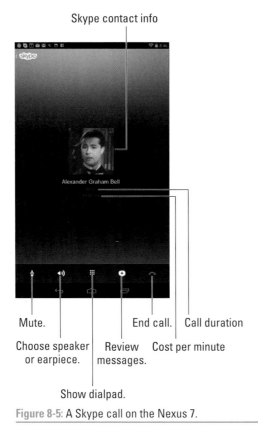

Mute.   End call.   Call duration

Choose speaker   Review   Cost per minute
or earpiece.   messages.

Show dialpad.

Figure 8-5: A Skype call on the Nexus 7.

5. To end the call, touch the red End Call button.

Refer to Figure 8-5 for the button's location.

To dial a number not associated with a contact, touch the Dialpad icon at the top of the main Skype screen, shown in the margin. Punch in the number to dial, starting with 1 (for the United States), the area code, then the number. Touch the green Dial button to place the call.

Lamentably, you can't receive a phone call using Skype on your Nexus 7 from a cell phone or landline unless you pay for a Skype online number. In that case, you can use Skype to both send and receive regular phone calls. This book doesn't cover the Online Number option.

✔ I recommend getting a good headset if you plan to use Skype often to place phone calls. If you do, ensure that you choose the Earpiece option from the Speaker button. (Refer to Figure 8-5.)

✔ In addition to having to pay the per-minute cost, you may be charged a connection fee for making the call.

✔ You can check the Skype website for a current list of call rates, for both domestic and international calls: www.skype.com.

✔ Unless you've paid Skype to have a specific phone number, the phone number shown on the recipient's Caller ID screen is something unexpected — often, merely the text Unknown. You might therefore want to e-mail the person you're calling and let her know that you're placing a Skype call. That way, the call won't be skipped because the Caller ID isn't recognized.

Part III
But Wait — There's More!

The 5th Wave   By Rich Tennant

"Okay, have we all signed in on our Nexus 7s?
Good. I see we have Barge, Teabag, Dink,
and Boob with us today."

In this part . . .

I love watching those magic-gadget commercials on TV. It doesn't matter what the gadget is or what it does — what's fun is the presentation. I especially enjoy the part where the announcer says, "But wait — there's more!" And then it ends with that person "doubling the offer" or throwing in some other gadget that you don't need for "free" or "for a limited time." Oh, and, "Hurry — operators are standing by."

The Nexus 7 could be sold in the manner of the do-it-all TV miracle gadget. You'll find a lot of "But wait — there's more!" when it comes to the many things the tablet can do. It's a map, a navigator, a picture book, a music player, an eBook reader, your personal calendar, an alarm clock, and so much more that I had to write this entire part of the book to explain it all.

Chapter 9

There's a Map for That

In This Chapter

▶ Exploring your world with Maps

▶ Adding layers to the map

▶ Finding your location

▶ Sharing your location

▶ Searching for places

▶ Using the Nexus 7 as a navigator

▶ Browsing the entire earth

Someday, the science fiction of teleportation will be a reality. It will be a boon to the transportation and tourist industries. And people will still complain about lost luggage.

One thing they probably won't complain about is being lost themselves. That's because they'll use the Nexus 70,000, a direct descendant of your Nexus 7. Using the Maps app, they'll be able to tell exactly where they are and even find interesting things nearby, such as some fine Canadian cuisine. Because it's the future, they might even be able to use the Nexus 70,000 to find their lost luggage.

A Map That Needs No Folding

Your location, as well as the location of things near and far, is found on the Nexus 7 by using the Maps app. Good news: You run no risk of improperly folding the Maps app. Better news: The Maps app charts the entire country, including freeways, highways, roads, streets, avenues, drives, bike paths, addresses, businesses, and points of interest.

Using the Maps app

You start the Maps app by choosing Maps from the All Apps screen. If you're starting the app for the first time or it has been recently updated, you can read its What's New screen; touch the OK button to continue.

The Nexus 7 communicates with global positioning system (GPS) satellites to hone in on your current location. (See the later sidebar "Activate your locations!") It's shown on the map, similar to Figure 9-1. The position is accurate to within a given range, as shown by a faint blue circle around your location on the map.

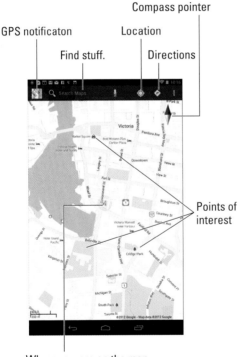

Compass pointer

GPS notificaton   Location

Find stuff.   Directions

Points of interest

Where you are on the map

Figure 9-1: Your location on a map.

Here are some fun things you can do when viewing the basic street map:

Zoom in: To make the map larger (to move it closer), double-tap the screen or spread your fingers on the touchscreen.

Zoom out: To make the map smaller (to see more), pinch your fingers on the touchscreen.

Pan and scroll: To see what's to the left or right or at the top or bottom of the map, drag your finger on the touchscreen; the map scrolls in the direction you drag your finger.

Rotate: Using two fingers, rotate the map clockwise or counter-clockwise. Touch the compass pointer (shown in Figure 9-1) to reorient the map with north at the top of the screen.

Perspective: Tap the Location button to switch to Perspective view, where the map is shown at an angle. Touch the Location button again (though now it's the Perspective button) to return to Flat-Map view, or, if that doesn't work, touch the compass pointer.

The closer you zoom in to the map, the more detail you see, such as street names, address block numbers, and businesses and other sites — but no tiny people.

🖚 The blue triangle (refer to Figure 9-1) shows in which general direction the tablet is pointing.

🖚 When the tablet's direction is unavailable, you see a blue dot as your location on the map.

🖚 When all you want is a virtual compass, similar to the one you lost as a kid, you can get a Compass app from the Google Play Store. See Chapter 12 for more information about the Google Play Store. Search for *compass*.

🖚 You can enter Perspective view for only your current location.

Adding layers

You add details from the Maps app by applying layers: A *layer* can enhance the map's visual appearance, provide more information, or add other fun features to the basic street map, such as the Satellite layer, shown in Figure 9-2.

The key to accessing layers is to touch the Menu icon button and choose the Layers command. Select an option from the Layers menu to add that information to the Map app's display.

Main roads

Your approximate location
and direction

Figure 9-2: The Satellite layer.

To remove the layer, choose it from the Layers menu; any active layer appears with a green check mark to its right. When a layer isn't applied, the street view appears.

✔ If you turn the Nexus 7 to a horizontal orientation, the Layers button appears in the upper-right area of the screen. Touch that button to quickly access the Layers menu.

✔ Only one layer can be viewed at a time.

✔ The Nexus 7 warns you whenever various applications access the tablet's Location feature. The warning is nothing serious — the tablet is simply letting you know that an app is accessing the device's physical location. Some folks may view this action as an invasion of privacy; hence the warnings. I see no issue with letting the tablet know where you are, but I understand that not everyone feels that way. If you'd rather not share location information, simply decline access when prompted.

Activate your locations!

The Maps app works best when you activate all the Nexus 7 location technology. I recommend that you turn on all the location settings. From the All Apps screen, open the Settings icon. Choose Location Services. On the Location Services screen, ensure that blue check marks appear by these two items:

Google's Location Service: Allows the tablet to use signals from nearby Wi-Fi and other types of wireless networks to help refine your position.

GPS Satellites: Allows your tablet to access the global positioning system (GPS) satellites, but it's not that accurate. That's why you need to activate more than this service to fully use your tablet's location abilities.

The third setting, Location & Google Search, has more to do with the tablet's response to your location than providing more accurate location information.

The location services work best when you've activated the Nexus 7's Wi-Fi networking. See Chapter 13 for information.

Find Things

The Maps app can help you find places in the real world, just like the Google app helps you find places on the Internet. Both operations work basically the same:

Open the Maps app and type something to find into the Search Maps text box, as illustrated earlier, in Figure 9-1. You can type a variety of terms into the Search box, as explained in this section.

Finding out where you are

The Maps app shows your location as a compass arrow or blue dot on the screen. But *where* is that? I mean, if you need to phone a tow truck, you can't say, "I'm the blue triangle on the gray slab by the green thing."

Well, you *can* say that, but it probably won't do any good.

To find your current street address, or any street address, long-press a location on the Maps screen. Up pops a bubble, similar to the one shown in Figure 9-3, that gives your approximate address.

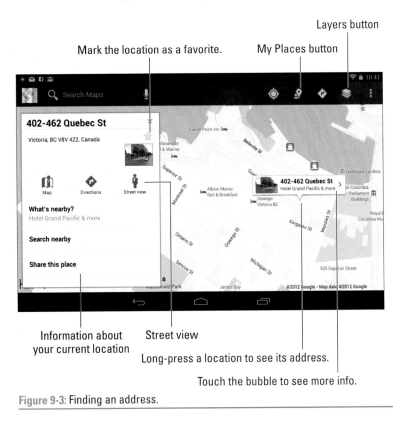

Mark the location as a favorite. My Places button Layers button

Information about your current location Street view

Long-press a location to see its address.

Touch the bubble to see more info.

Figure 9-3: Finding an address.

If you touch the address bubble, you see a pop-up window full of interesting things you can do, also shown in Figure 9-3.

- ✔ This trick works only when the tablet has Internet access. If Internet access isn't available, the Maps app is unable to communicate with the Google map servers.

- ✔ When you're searching for a location, distance and general direction are shown in the pop-up window. Otherwise, as shown in Figure 9-3, the distance and direction information isn't necessary.

- ✔ The What's Nearby command displays a list of nearby businesses or points of interest, some of them shown on the screen and others available if you touch the What's Nearby command.

✔ Choose the Search Nearby item to use the Search command to locate businesses, people, or points of interest near the given location.

✔ What's *really* fun to play with is the Street View command. Choosing it displays the location from a 360-degree perspective. In Street view, you can browse a locale, pan and tilt, or zoom in on details to familiarize yourself with an area, for example — whether you're familiarizing yourself with a location or planning a burglary.

Looking for a specific address

To locate an address, type it into the Search box; for example:

```
1313 N. Harbor Blvd., Anaheim, CA 92803
```

Touch the Search button on the keyboard, and that location is then shown on the map. The next step is getting directions, which you can read about in the later section "Getting directions."

✔ You don't need to type the entire address. Oftentimes, all you need is the street number and street name and then either the city name or zip code.

✔ If you omit the city name or zip code, the Nexus 7 looks for the closest matching address near your current location.

Finding a business, restaurant, or point of interest

You may not know an address, but you know when you crave sushi or Hungarian or perhaps the exotic flavors of Canada. Maybe you need a hotel or a gas station, or you have to find a place that buys old dentures. To find a business entity or a point of interest, type its name in the Search box; for example:

```
Movie theater
```

This command flags movie theaters on the current Maps screen or nearby.

Specify your current location, as described earlier in this chapter, to find locations near you. Otherwise, the Maps app looks for places near the area you see on the screen.

Or you can be specific and look for businesses near a certain location by specifying the city name, district, or zip code, such as

```
Booze 02554
```

After typing this command and touching the Search button, you see a smattering of tippling establishments found near Nantucket, Massachusetts, similar to the ones shown in Figure 9-4.

Search results

Search text

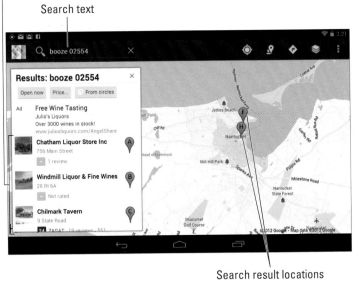

Search result locations

Figure 9-4: Finding drinking establishments near Nantucket.

To see more information about a result, touch it; touch either the item in the search results list or the "pin" that's dropped on the map, such as item F in Figure 9-4. You see a pop-up cartoon bubble, which you can touch to get even more specific information.

You can touch the Directions button on the restaurant's (or any location's) details screen to get directions; see the later section "Getting directions."

- ✔ Every letter or dot on the screen represents a search result. (Refer to Figure 9-4.)
- ✔ Spread your fingers on the touchscreen to zoom in to the map.

✔ You can create a contact for the location, keeping it as a part of your Contacts list: After touching the location balloon, touch the Menu icon button and choose the command Add As a Contact. The contact is created using data that's known about the business, including its location and tablet number and even a web page address — if that information is available.

Searching for favorite or recent places

The Maps app lets you search for things in the real world just like the Chrome app lets you find stuff on the Internet. And just as you can bookmark favorite websites on the Internet, you can mark favorite places in the real world. It's the Maps app feature called My Places.

To visit your favorite places or browse your recent map searches, touch the Menu icon button and choose the My Places command. You can also touch the My Places button, shown in the margin, when you view the Map app horizontally.

The My Places window sports three different categories of places you've starred (marked as favorites), locations you've recently searched for, or items saved for offline searches.

✔ The Starred list shows your favorite locations. Mark a location as a favorite by touching the Star button when you view the location's details. If the Star button doesn't appear, touch the Menu icon button and choose the Add Star command.

✔ The Recent list allows you to peruse items you've located or searched for recently.

✔ The Offline list shows those portions of the globe you've selected and stored so that you can peruse their details in the Maps app when an Internet connection isn't available.

Touch the X button to close the My Places window when you're done using it.

Locating a contact's address

You can hone in on where your friends in the People app dwell by using the Maps app. This trick works when you've specified an address for the contact — home, work, prison, or another location. If so, the Nexus 7 can easily help you find that location or even give you directions.

The secret? Touch the contact's address in the People app. In mere moments, you see the contact's location displayed.

The first time you're presented with locating a contact's address, you may see the Complete Action Using window. My advice is to choose the Maps app. Touch the Always button, and you'll never be bothered by the prompt again.

Nexus 7 the Navigator

Finding something is only half the job. The other half is getting there. The Nexus 7 is ever ready, thanks to the various direction and navigation features nestled in the Maps app.

I don't believe that the Nexus 7 has a car mount, not like a cell phone does. Therefore, if you use your tablet in your auto, I strongly recommend that you have someone else hold it and read the directions. Or use voice navigation and, for goodness' sake, don't look at the tablet while you're driving!

Getting directions

One command that's associated with locations on the map is Get Directions. Here's how to use it:

1. **Touch the Directions button in a location's cartoon bubble.**

   Or you may see the Directions button when you display details about a location. The Directions button icon is shown in the margin.

   After touching the Directions button, you see the pop-up window shown in Figure 9-5. It's preset to help you get to the location you chose in Step 1 from your current location. You can change the My Location item to any other address or swap the items, as illustrated in the figure.

   If you don't see the Directions button, long-press a location. Choose the item Get Directions from the menu that appears. Skip to Step 3.

2. **Ensure that the starting location and destination are what you want.**

   If they're backward, touch the Swap button. (Refer to Figure 9-5.) You can touch the Bookmark button to choose a favorite place, a contact, or a specific map location.

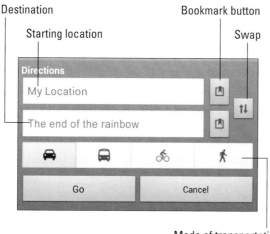

Destination

Starting location

Bookmark button

Swap

Mode of transportation

Figure 9-5: Getting where you want to go.

3. Choose a method of transportation.

The available options vary, depending on your location. In Figure 9-5, the items are (from left to right) Car, Public Transportation, Bicycle, and On Foot.

4. Touch the Go button.

A list of directions appears on the left side of the screen. On the right side of the screen you see your route plotted out as a blue line on the map.

If you can't constantly look at the tablet to see the map, touch the Navigation button, shown in the margin. Also see the next section for more details on navigation using the Maps app.

✓ Tilt the tablet sideways (to the horizontal orientation) to make the onscreen map and directions more useful.

✓ A summary of the distance journey and travel time appears in the Directions box on the left side of the screen.

✓ You can modify your journey by dragging the blue line around with your finger. Touch one of the waypoints, shown in the margin, to drag the route to other streets or nearby highways. The journey distance and travel time adjust themselves as you change your route.

✓ The Maps app alerts you to any toll roads on the specified route. As you travel, you can choose alternative, non-toll routes, if they're available. You're prompted to switch routes during navigation; see the next section.

✓ You may not get perfect directions from the Maps app, but for places you've never visited, it's a useful tool.

Navigating to your destination

Maps and lists of directions are so 20th century. I don't know why anyone would bother, especially when the Nexus 7 features a digital copilot, in the form of voice navigation.

To use navigation, choose the Navigation option from any list of directions. Or touch the Navigation button, shown in the margin. You can also enter the Navigation app directly by choosing it from the All Apps screen, though then you must type (or speak) your destination, so it's easier to start in the Maps app.

In Navigation mode, the Nexus 7 displays an interactive map that shows your current location and turn-by-turn directions for reaching your destination. A digital voice tells you how far to go and when to turn, for example, and gives you other nagging advice — just like a backseat driver, albeit an accurate one.

After choosing Navigation, sit back and have the tablet dictate your directions. You can simply listen, or glance at the tablet for an update of where you're heading.

To stop navigation, touch the Menu icon button and choose the Exit Navigation command.

✓ To remove the navigation route from the screen, exit Navigation mode and return to the Maps app. Touch the Menu icon button and choose the Clear Map command.

✓ When you tire of hearing the navigation voice, touch the Menu icon button and choose the Turn Off Voice command.

✓ I refer to the navigation voice as *Gertrude*.

✓ The neat thing about the Navigation feature is that whenever you screw up, a new course is immediately calculated.

✓ In Navigation mode, the Nexus 7 consumes a lot of battery power. I highly recommend that you plug the tablet into your car's power adapter ("cigarette lighter") for the duration of the trip. Any Android cell phone power adapter works, as does any adapter with a micro-USB connector.

Chapter 10

Name That Tune

The Nexus 7's amazing arsenal of features includes its ability to play music. So it effectively replaces any gramophone that you've been lugging around, which is the whole idea behind an all-in-one gizmo like the Nexus 7. You can cheerfully and adeptly transfer all your old Edison cylinders and 78 LPs to the Nexus 7 for your listening enjoyment. More specifically, this chapter explains how to listen to music, get more music, and manage that music on your tablet.

Listen Here

Your source of musical delight on the Nexus 7 is the app aptly named Play Music. You can find the app on the All Apps screen or use the shortcut that dwells on the Favorites bar at the bottom of the Home screen.

Browsing your music library

After you start the Play Music app, you see a screen similar to Figure 10-1. If you're displeased with the quantity of available music, refer to the later section "Add Some Music to Your Life." It explains how to get more tunes.

The music stored on your Nexus 7 is presented in the Play Music app by category. Each category appears atop the screen. (Refer to Figure 10-1.) Change categories by swiping the screen left or right.

Categories   Google Play Store

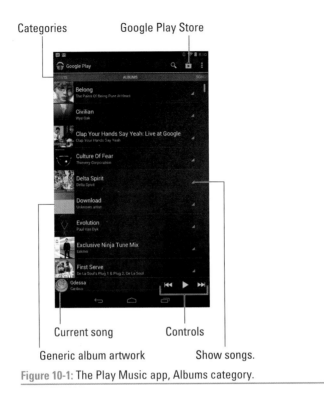

Current song   Controls

Generic album artwork   Show songs.

Figure 10-1: The Play Music app, Albums category.

Here are the categories used in the Play Music app:

Playlists: Music you've organized into playlists that you create. Choose a playlist name to view songs organized in that playlist. Included are recently played songs, songs from the Internet, and other preset categories.

Recent: Songs and albums are listed in the order you've imported from your computer or purchased online. Scroll the list up or down to find recent items.

Artists: Songs listed by recording artist or group. Choose Artist to see those songs listed by album.

Albums: Music organized by album, as shown in Figure 10-1. Choose an album to list its songs.

Songs: All music (songs and audio) listed individually in alphabetical order.

Genres: Audio organized by categories such as Alternative, Country, and Rock.

These categories are merely ways the music is organized — ways to make the music easier to find when you may know an artist's name but not an album title. The Genres category is for those times when you're in a mood for a certain type of music but don't know, or don't mind, who recorded it.

A *playlist* is a list you create yourself to organize songs by favorite, theme, mood, or whatever other characteristic you want. The section "Organize Your Music," later in this chapter, discusses playlists.

- ✒ Music is stored on the Nexus 7's internal memory.

- ✒ The size of the internal memory limits the total amount of music that can be stored on your tablet. Also, consider that storing pictures and videos horns in on some of the space that can be used to store music.

- ✒ Two types of album artwork are used by the Play Music app. For purchased music, the album artwork represents the original album. That may also happen for music copied (*imported*) from your computer. Otherwise, the Play Music app slaps down a generic album cover, as shown in Figure 10-1.

- ✒ There's no easy or obvious way to apply album cover artwork to music with a generic album cover.

- ✒ When the Nexus 7 can't recognize an artist, it uses the title *Unknown Artist.* It usually happens with music you copy manually to your tablet, but it can also apply to audio recordings you make yourself.

Playing a tune

To listen to music by locating a song in the Play Music app library, as described in the preceding section, touch the song title, and the song plays, as shown in Figure 10-2.

While the song plays, you're free to do anything else on the Nexus 7. In fact, the song continues to play even when the tablet is locked or goes to sleep.

After the song is done playing, the next song in the list plays. The list order depends on how you start the song. For example, if you start a song from Album view, all songs in that album play in the order listed.

The next song in the list doesn't play if you have activated the Shuffle button. (See Figure 10-2.) In that case, the Play Music app randomly chooses another song from the same list. Who knows which one is next?

The next song also might not play when you have the Repeat option on: The three repeat settings are illustrated in Table 10-1, along with the shuffle settings. To change settings, simply touch either the Shuffle or Repeat button. If these buttons disappear from the screen, touch the screen briefly, and they'll show up again.

Table 10-1		Shuffle and Repeat Button Icons
Icon	*Setting*	*What Happens When You Touch the Icon*
⤬	No Shuffle	Songs play one after the other.
⤬	Shuffle	Songs are played in random order.
⇄	No Repeat	Songs don't repeat.
⇄①	Single Repeat	The same song plays over and over.
⇄	List Repeat	All songs in the list play over and over.

To stop the song from playing, touch the Pause button. (See Figure 10-2.)

A notification icon appears while music is playing on the Nexus 7, as shown in the margin. To quickly summon the Play Music app and see which song is playing, or to pause the song, touch that notification, or pop up the notifications list, to see the name of the song that's playing. You can use the controls in the notification to pause the song or to skip forward or backward.

  ✔ The volume is set by using the Volume switch on the side of the Nexus 7.

  ✔ While browsing the Play Music app's library, you see the currently playing song displayed at the bottom of the screen, as shown in Figure 10-1.

Album cover artwork   Song info

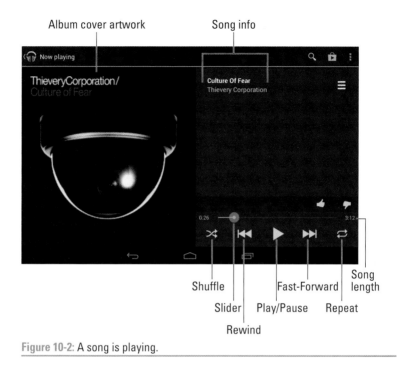

Shuffle   Fast-Forward   Song length

Slider   Play/Pause   Repeat

Rewind

Figure 10-2: A song is playing.

✔ Most of the music on your Nexus 7 is Google music, originating from the Internet. It's not available to play unless the tablet has a Wi-Fi connection. See the later section "Making music available full-time" for a tip on how to remedy this situation.

✔ To choose which songs play after each other, create a playlist. See the section "Organize Your Music," later in this chapter.

✔ After the last song in the list plays, the Play Music app stops playing songs — unless you have set the List Repeat option, in which case the list plays again.

✔ You can use the Nexus 7's search abilities to help locate tunes in your Music library. You can search by artist name, song title, or album. The key is to touch the Search icon button when you're using the Play Music app. Type all or part of the text you're searching for, and touch the Search button on the onscreen keyboard. Choose the song you want to hear from the list that's displayed.

"What's this song?"

The Nexus 7 comes with a special widget. It's called What's This Song. You can install it from the All Apps screen onto the Home screen, as described in Chapter 16. From the Home screen, you can use the What's This Song widget to identify music playing within earshot of your tablet.

To use the widget, touch it on the Home screen. The widget immediately starts listening to your surroundings, as shown in the middle of the sidebar figure. After a few seconds, the song is recognized and displayed. You can choose to either buy the song at the Google Play Store or touch the Refresh button and start over.

The What's This Song widget works best (exclusively, I would argue) with recorded music. Try as you might, you cannot sing into the thing and have it recognize a song. Humming doesn't work, either. I've tried playing the guitar and piano and — nope — that didn't work either. But for listening to ambient music, it's a good tool for telling what you're listening to.

Being the life of the party

You need to do four things to make your Nexus 7 the soul of your next shindig or soirée:

- ✓ Connect it to a stereo.
- ✓ Use the Shuffle command.
- ✓ Set the Repeat command.
- ✓ Provide plenty of drinks and snacks.

Hook the Nexus 7 into any stereo that has a standard line input. You need, on one end, an audio cable that has a mini-headphone jack and, on the other end, an audio input that matches your stereo. Look for such a cable at Radio Shack or any stereo store.

After you connect your tablet, start the Play Music app and choose the party playlist you've created. If you want the songs to play in random order, touch the Shuffle button.

You might also consider choosing the List Repeat command (see Table 10-1) so that all songs in the playlist repeat.

To play all songs saved on your Nexus 7, choose the Songs category and touch the first song in the list. You should also consider creating a playlist, just in case not everyone likes *all* your tunes. See the later section "Organize Your Music."

Enjoy your party, and please drink responsibly.

Add Some Music to Your Life

My Nexus 7 came with a paltry selection of tunes, mostly available through Google Play on the Internet. Otherwise, none of my favorites was in there! What to do? Why, add more music! This section goes over a few ways to get music into your tablet.

Buying music at the Google Play Store

It's possible to get your music for your Nexus 7 from the same source where you get apps for your Nexus 7 — the Google Play Store. Getting apps is covered in Chapter 12. Getting music is covered right here:

1. **Ensure that your tablet has a Wi-Fi connection.**

   The Google Play Store is an Internet thing. You need Internet access to browse and buy music.

2. **Open the Play Store app.**

   It can be found on the Home screen, on the far right end of the Favorites bar. You can also get to the Google Play Music store by touching the Play Store button in the Play Music app. (Refer to Figure 10-1.)

3. **Choose the Music category.**

   The Music category is shown on the main screen. If necessary, touch the App button in the upper-left corner of the screen until you see the main screen.

4. **Use the Search icon button to locate music you want, or just browse the categories.**

   Keep an eye out for free music offers at the Play Store. It's a great way to pick up some tunes.

   Eventually, you see a page showing details about the song or album. Choose a song from the list to hear a preview.

The button next to the song or album indicates the purchase price, or it says *FREE*, for free music.

5. Touch the price button to purchase a song or album.

Don't worry: You're not buying anything yet.

6. Choose your credit card or payment source.

If no credit card or payment source appears, similar to the one shown in Figure 10-3, choose the Add Card option to add a payment method. Sign up with Google Checkout and submit your credit card or other payment information.

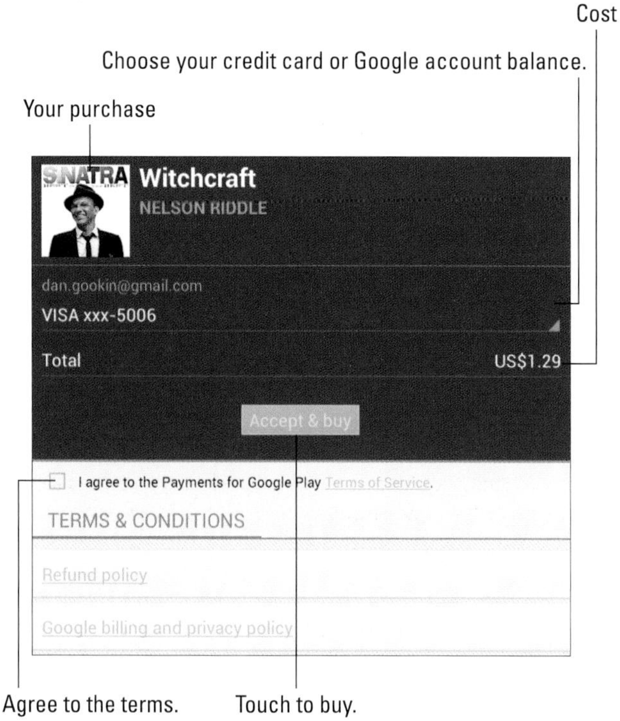

Cost

Choose your credit card or Google account balance.

Your purchase

S.NATRA Witchcraft
NELSON RIDDLE

dan.gookin@gmail.com
VISA xxx-5006

Total   US$1.29

Accept & buy

☐ I agree to the Payments for Google Play Terms of Service.

TERMS & CONDITIONS

Refund policy

Google billing and privacy policy

Agree to the terms.   Touch to buy.

Figure 10-3: Buying some music.

7. Touch the Accept & Buy button.

If the Accept & Buy button isn't available (refer to Figure 10-3), you have to touch the check box to agree to the terms.

The album or song is downloaded into your tablet.

"Can I copy music from my PC to the Nexus 7?"

It's possible to import music from your PC into the Nexus 7. The file transfer works okay, and Chapter 14 offers information on making the connection and copying files. I suggest that you not even try.

That's because the traditional way to exchange files between a computer and a mobile music device is to use a jukebox program on your computer, something that manages music. Such programs are designed to interface with portable devices and quickly copy your music over to them.

The problem is that the Play Music app doesn't recognize the Windows Media Audio (WMA) file format used to store music in the Windows Media Player program. Other Android devices, but not the Nexus 7, may let you play your WMA files, which means that you can copy over your music library but the tablet won't recognize or play any of your songs.

One possible solution is to copy only files in the MP3 audio format. But Windows doesn't natively store music in this file format. So you're kind of screwed when it comes to sharing music between your computer and the Nexus 7. Blame Google, not me.

A notification appears when the album or song has completed the transfer. You can then use the Play Music app to listen to the new music; you'll find it quickly by choosing the Recent category from the Play Music app's main screen.

- ✓ All music sales are final. Don't blame me — I'm just writing down Google's current policy for music purchases.

- ✓ The Google Play Music notification icon is the same that appears when you download a new app for your phone. The notification name, however, is Google Play Music.

- ✓ You'll eventually receive a Gmail notice regarding the purchase. The Gmail message lists a summary of your purchase.

Album artwork for your imported songs

When you import music into the Nexus 7, it's often missing one key thing: the album art. Instead of the bitchin' classic cover, you see a generic piece of bland artwork that even Percy Faith wouldn't put on one of his records. But all is not lost!

You can add album art, providing you're a bit more adept at using computers than the typical human. The album artwork needs to be saved in a file named albumart.jpg (where jpg is the JPEG file type). Copy that file to the folder where your music is stored on the Nexus 7. So if you have a folder full of Percy Faith's easy-listening music, you save the albumart.jpg file into that folder.

See Chapter 14 for information on working with files and folders on the Nexus 7, as well as how to copy files between your computer and the tablet.

Using the Internet to access your tunes

Music you purchase from the Google Play Music store is available on any mobile Android device with the Play Music app installed as long as you use the same Google account on that device. You can also listen to your tunes by visiting the music.google.com site on any computer connected to the Internet.

As long as you log in to your Google account on a computer connected to the Internet, you can use Google Play on the Internet to buy music, listen to music, and even upload music from your computer into your Google Play music library.

Organize Your Music

The Play Music app categorizes your music by album, artist, song, and so forth, but unless you have only one album and enjoy all the songs on it, that configuration probably won't do. To better organize your music, you can create *playlists.* That way, you can hear the music you want to hear, in the order you want, for whatever mood hits you.

Reviewing your playlists

Any playlists that you've already created, or that have been preset on the tablet, appear in the Playlists category, which you can choose by swiping the categories list all the way to the left in the Play Music app. (Refer to Figure 10-1.) Playlists you've created are displayed on the screen, as shown in Figure 10-4.

Categories

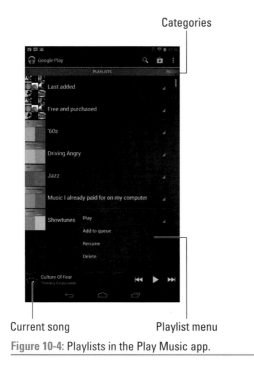

Current song   Playlist menu

Figure 10-4: Playlists in the Play Music app.

To see which songs are in a playlist, touch the playlist album icon. To play the songs in the playlist, touch the first song in the list. Or you can choose the Play command from the playlist's menu, as shown in Figure 10-4.

A playlist is a helpful way to organize music when a song's information may not have been completely imported into the Nexus 7. For example, if you're like me, you probably have a lot of songs labeled *Unknown.* A quick way to remedy this situation is to name a playlist after the artist and then add those unknown songs to the playlist. The next section describes how it's done.

Creating your own playlists

Making a new playlist is easy, and adding songs to the playlist is even easier. Follow these steps:

1. Choose the Playlist category in the Play Music app.

2. **Touch the Menu icon button in the upper-right corner of the screen.**

3. **Choose New Playlist.**

4. **Type a name for your playlist.**

   Short and descriptive names are best.

5. **Touch the OK button to create the playlist.**

   The new playlist is created and placed onto the Playlists screen, similar to the one shown in Figure 10-4.

But the playlist is empty! To add songs, you go out and fetch them, adding each one to a playlist. Here's how you do that:

1. **Hunt down the song you want to add to a playlist.**

   You don't need to play the song. Simply display the song in the Play Music app.

   Likewise, you can hunt down albums, artists, or even genres. The technique described in this set of steps works for every category in the Play Music app.

2. **Touch the menu triangle by the song (or album or artist).**

3. **Choose the Add to Playlist command.**

4. **Choose a playlist.**

   The song (or album or artist) is added to the playlist's repertoire of music.

Repeat this set of steps to continue adding songs to playlists.

You can have as many playlists as you like on the Nexus 7 and stick as many songs as you like into them. Adding songs to a playlist doesn't noticeably affect the tablet's storage capacity.

  ✓ To remove a song from a playlist, open the playlist and touch the menu triangle by the song. Choose the Remove from Playlist command.

  ✓ Removing a song from a playlist doesn't delete the song from the Nexus 7's music library.

  ✓ Songs in a playlist can be rearranged: While viewing the playlist, use the tab on the far left end of a song title to drag that song up or down in the list.

  ✓ To delete a playlist, touch the menu triangle in the playlist icon's lower-right corner. (Refer to Figure 10-4.) Choose the Delete command. Touch OK to confirm.

Making music available full-time

Because Google made it a pain to copy music to your Nexus 7 from your PC, most of the music stored on the tablet is from the Internet. As long as you have a Wi-Fi connection on your Nexus 7, the music plays. When you don't have a connection, the music doesn't, either. That is, unless you follow these steps:

1. **Locate the song, artist, or album you want to keep stored on the tablet.**

2. **Touch the Menu button to the right of the song, artist, or album.**

3. **Choose the Keep on Device command.**

    The Nexus 7 ensures that the music is transferred to the tablet from the Internet and therefore is available to play all the time.

A quick way to select multiple songs, albums, or artists for download from the Internet is to touch the Menu icon button and choose the command Choose On-Device Music. Touch the push-pin icon next to the songs you want to keep on the tablet. Touch the check mark button (in the lower-left area of the screen) when you're done.

If you want to see which songs are available on the device, touch the Menu icon button and choose the On Device Only option. After doing so, only the music copied to your Nexus 7 appears in the Play Music app. Choose the On Device Only command again to see all your music, stored locally (on the Nexus 7's internal storage) or online.

Removing unwanted music

Depending on the source, you have two ways to deal with unwanted music on your Nexus 7.

The first way is to visit Google Play on the Internet at `https://music.google.com`. Click the menu button by a song and choose the Delete command. Click the Delete Song button to confirm.

The steps for removing music stored directly on the Nexus 7 are similar: Touch the menu button by a song and choose the Delete command. Touch the OK button to confirm.

✔ When you don't see the Delete command on the Nexus 7, the song cannot be removed locally. Visit Google Play on the Internet to remove the song.

- There's no way to recover a song you delete on the Nexus 7.

- Removing music stored on the tablet occupies the Nexus 7's internal storage. If that's a concern, refer to the previous section, which talks about storing music locally. You can repeat the steps in that section to remove the Keep On Device option for music, which frees up storage space.

Music from the Stream

Though they're not broadcast radio stations, some sources on the Internet — *Internet radio* sites — play music. Lamentably, the Nexus 7 comes with no Internet radio apps, but that doesn't stop you from finding a few good ones at the Google Play Store. Two free services that I can recommend are

- TuneIn Radio
- Pandora Radio

The TuneIn Radio app gives you access to hundreds of Internet radio stations broadcasting around the world. They're organized by category, so you can find just about whatever you want. Many of the radio stations are also broadcast radio stations, so odds are good that you can find a local station or two, which you can listen to on your Nexus 7.

Pandora Radio lets you select music based on your mood, and it customizes, according to your feedback, the tunes you listen to. The app works like the Internet site www.pandora.com, in case you're familiar with it. The nifty thing about Pandora is that the more you listen, the better the app gets at finding music you like.

All these apps are available at the Google Play Store. They're free, though paid versions might also be available.

- You need a Wi-Fi connection if you plan on listening to music streaming from the Internet.

- See Chapter 12 for more information about the Google Play Store.

- Internet music of the type delivered by the apps mentioned in this section is referred to by the nerds as *streaming* music. That's because the music arrives on your Nexus 7 as a continuous download from the source. Unlike music you download and save, streaming music is played as it comes in and isn't stored long-term.

Chapter 11

Other Amazing Feats

Most gizmos are designed to solve a single problem. The food processor slices, grates, or chops food, but it doesn't play music (though I'm sure that John Cage would argue this point). The lawn mower is good at cutting the grass but terrible at telling time. And if you have a tuba, it can play music, but it's a poor substitute for a hair dryer. That's all well and good because people accept limitations on devices designed for a specific purpose.

The Nexus 7 is a gizmo with many purposes. Its abilities are limited only by the apps you get for it. To help you grasp this concept, the tablet comes with a slate of apps preinstalled. They can give you an idea of what the tablet is capable of, or you can simply use those apps to make the Nexus 7 a more versatile and useful device.

It's a Clock

Your Nexus 7 keeps constant, accurate track of the time, which is displayed at the top of the Home screen as well as on the lock screen. That's handy, but it just isn't enough, so the tablet ships with the Clock app.

Start the Clock app from the All Apps screen to witness the time displayed, big-size, on your Nexus 7. As a bonus, you can also see the day and date. That's handy, but it just isn't enough, so you can set alarms as well. Yes, the Nexus 7 can be your alarm clock.

To set an alarm, touch the Set Alarm button, illustrated in Figure 11-1. You see a list of current alarms — plus, an Add Alarm button, used to create new alarms. The process works like this:

Timer Clock Stopwatch

Add alarm

Activate alarm

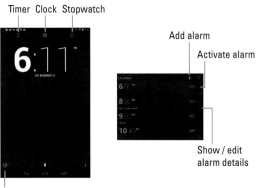

Show / edit
alarm details

Set alarm

Figure 11-1: The Clock app.

1. **Touch the Add Alarm button in the Alarms window.**

   The Set Alarm keypad appears.

2. **Enter a time for the alarm, including AM or PM.**

3. **Touch the OK button.**

   The alarm appears in the list, expanded for editing. The On switch is active, meaning that the alarm is set.

4. **Place a blue check mark by the Repeat option to set the alarm's frequency.**

   Touch those days of the week on which you want the alarm to sound.

   To have the alarm sound only once (when set), don't put a blue check mark by the Repeat option.

5. **Choose Ringtone item to specify which sound plays for the alarm.**

   The Ringtone item displays the name of the current ring-tone, such as Cesium or whatever-ium.

6. **Touch the up-pointing chevron to save your changes and close the Alarm's information screen.**

The alarm is set and ready to trigger according to the options you've chosen.

Alarms must be set or else they don't trigger. Touch the Off button to set an alarm. Set alarms appear with the On button active.

When the alarm goes off, you can touch the Dismiss button to tell the tablet, "Okay! I'm up!" Or you can touch the Snooze button to be annoyed again after ten minutes.

✔ Information about a set alarm appears on the Clock app's screen as well as on the Nexus 7's lock screen.

✔ When an alarm is set, the Alarm notification appears in the Status area atop the screen, as shown in the margin. It's your all-the-time clue that an alarm is set and ready to trigger.

✔ The Snooze duration is set by touching the Menu icon button at the top of the Alarms screen. (Refer to Figure 11-1.) Choose Settings, then Snooze Length. It's normally ten minutes.

✔ To edit an alarm, choose it from the Alarms screen.

✔ Turning off an alarm doesn't delete the alarm.

✔ To remove an alarm, long-press it and touch the Trash icon at the top of the screen.

✔ The alarm doesn't work when you turn off the Nexus 7. The alarm does, however, go off when the tablet is locked.

It's a Large Calculator

The Calculator is perhaps the oldest of all computer programs. Even my stupid cell phone, back in the 1990s, had a calculator program. (I won't dignify it by calling it an "app.")

Start the Calculator app by choosing its icon from the All Apps screen. The Calculator appears, as shown in Figure 11-2.

Scary calculator buttons

Clear/Delete button

Typical calculator buttons

Figure 11-2: The Calculator.

Type your equations using the various buttons on the screen. The parentheses buttons can help you determine which part of a long equation gets calculated first. Use the Clr button to clear input.

✔ Long-press the calculator's text (or results) to cut or copy the results.

✔ The Clear (CLR) button changes to the Delete button when you type a number. That way, you can delete your input without clearing out the entire calculation.

✔ I use the Calculator most often to determine my tip at a restaurant. In Figure 11-2, a calculation is being made for an 18 percent tip on an $89.56 tab.

It's a Calendar

Feel free to take any datebook you have and throw it away. You never need to buy another one again. That's because your Nexus 7 is the ideal datebook and appointment calendar. Thanks to the Calendar app and the Google Calendar service on the Internet, you can manage all your scheduling right on your Nexus 7. It's almost cinchy.

✔ Google Calendar works with your Google account to keep track of your schedule and appointments. You can visit Google Calendar on the web at

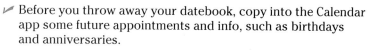
```
http://calendar.google.com
```

✔ You automatically have Google Calendar; it comes with your Google account.

✔ I recommend that you use the Calendar app on your Nexus 7 to access Google Calendar. It's a better way to access your schedule than using the Chrome app to reach Google Calendar on the web.

✔ Before you throw away your datebook, copy into the Calendar app some future appointments and info, such as birthdays and anniversaries.

Browsing your schedule

To see what's happening next, to peruse upcoming important events, or to simply know which day of the month it is, summon the Calendar app. It's located on the All Apps screen along with all the other apps that dwell on your Nexus 7. A shortcut can also be found in the Google folder on the far left side of the Favorites bar on the Home screen.

Figure 11-3 shows the Calendar app's three views: Month, Week, and Day. There's also Agenda view, which displays only upcoming events. Each view is chosen from the View menu, illustrated in Figure 11-3.

✔ Use Month view to see an overview of what's going on, and use Week view or Day view to see your appointments.

✔ I check Week view at the start of the week to remind me of what's coming up.

✔ To scroll from month to month, swipe the screen up or down. In Week view and Day view, scroll from left to right.

✔ Touch the Today button to be instantly whisked back to the current day.

✔ A black bar appears across the current day, indicating the current time.

✔ See the later section "Creating a new event" for information on reviewing and creating events.

✔ Different colors flag your events, as shown in Figure 11-3. The colors represent a calendar category to which the events are assigned. See the later section "Creating a new event" for information on calendar categories.

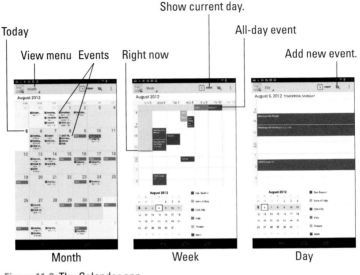

Figure 11-3: The Calendar app.

Reviewing appointments

To see more detail about an event, touch it. When you're using Month view, touch the date with the event on it to see Week view. Then choose an event to see its details, similar to the event shown in Figure 11-4.

The information you see depends on how much information was recorded when the event was created. Some events have only a minimum of information; others may have details, such as a location for the event. When the event's location is listed, you can touch the location and the Maps app pops up to show you where the event is being held.

Touch the Back navigation button to dismiss the event's details.

✔ Birthdays and a few other events on the calendar may be pulled from the People app or even from some social networking apps. That probably explains why some events can be listed twice; they're pulled in from two sources.

✔ The best way to review upcoming appointments is to choose the Agenda item from the View menu.

✔ There's also a Calendar widget that you can set down on the Home screen. As in Agenda view, the widget displays only a

list of your upcoming appointments. See Chapter 16 for information on applying widgets to the tablet's Home screen.

✔ The Google Now feature on the Nexus 7 also lists any immediate appointments or events. See the later section "It's Google
Now."

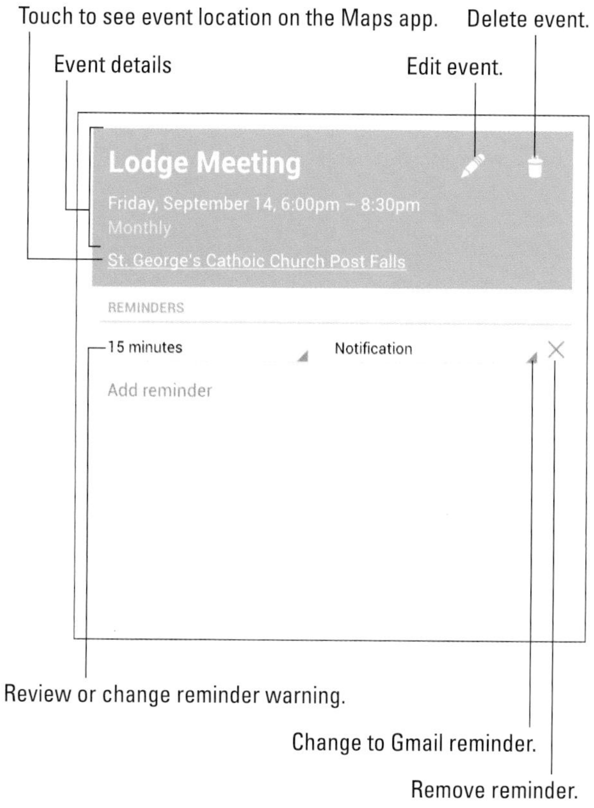

Touch to see event location on the Maps app.   Delete event.

Event details   Edit event.

> **Lodge Meeting**
>
> Friday, September 14, 6:00pm – 8:30pm
> Monthly
> St. George's Cathoic Church Post Falls

REMINDERS

15 minutes   ◢   Notification   ◢   ✕

Add reminder

Review or change reminder warning.

Change to Gmail reminder.

Remove reminder.

Figure 11-4: Event details.

Creating a new event

The key to making the calendar work is to add events: appointments, things to do, meetings, or full-day events such as birthdays
or colonoscopies. To create a new event, follow these steps in the
Calendar app:

1. Select the day for the event.

Or if you like, you can switch to Day view, where you can
touch the starting time for the new event.

2. Touch the Add New Event button. (Refer to Figure 11-3.)

The New Event screen appears. Your job now is to fill in the blanks to create the new event.

The more information you supply, the more detailed the event, and the more you can do with it on your Nexus 7 as well as on Google Calendar on the Internet.

3. Choose a calendar category for the event.

Touch the colored calendar text atop the screen to choose a calendar category.

Calendar categories are handy because they let you organize and color-code your events. They're confusing because Google calls them "calendars." I think of them more as categories. So I have different calendars (categories) for my personal and work schedules, government duties, clubs, and so on.

4. Type an event name.

Sometimes, I simply write the name of the person I'm meeting.

5. Type a location for the event in the Where field.

Adding an event location not only tells you where the event will be located but also hooks that information into the Maps app. My advice is to type information into the event's Where field just as though you're typing information to search for in the Maps app. When the event is displayed, the location is a link; touch the link to see where it is on a map.

6. Set the meeting duration.

Because you followed Step 1, you don't have to set the date (unless the event is longer than a day). Touch the time menu buttons, if necessary, to adjust when the event starts and stops.

When the event lasts all day, such as a birthday or your mother-in-law's visit that was supposed to last for an hour, touch the All Day check mark.

7. Specify whether the event repeats.

Touch the Repeat button to set up a recurring schedule. For example, if your meeting is held every month on the third Wednesday, touch the menu button by the Repetition item and choose that option.

When you have events that repeat twice a month — say, on the first and third Mondays — you need to create two separate events, one for the first Monday and another for the third. Then have each event repeat monthly.

8. Set whether the event has a reminder.

The Calendar app is configured to automatically set a reminder ten minutes before an event begins. If you prefer not to have a reminder, touch the X button by the Reminders item to remove the reminder.

You can set additional reminders by touching the Add Reminder button. Change the reminder time by touching the menu button and choosing a new time value.

Reminders come in two flavors: notifications as well as Gmail messages.

9. Fill in other fields, if you like.

10. Touch the Done button to create the new event.

The Done button has a check mark by it, and it's located in the upper-right corner of the New Event screen.

The new event appears on the calendar, reminding you that you need to do something on such-and-such a day.

✔ You can change an event at any time: Simply touch the event to bring up more information and then touch Choose Edit from the top of the screen to modify the event. (Refer to Figure 11-4.)

✔ To remove an event, touch the event to bring up more information, and touch the Delete button in the upper-right area of the screen. Touch the OK button to confirm.

✔ It's best to work with and manage the various calendar categories using a computer to access the Google Calendar website. You can view and select your various calendar categories from within the Calendar app: Touch the Menu icon button and choose the Settings command. Choose your Gmail account to see the list of calendars available. You can add or remove blue check marks to show or hide the various calendar categories.

✔ It's necessary to set an event's time zone only when it takes place in another time zone or when an event spans time zones, such as an airline flight. In that case, the Calendar app automatically adjusts the starting and stopping times for events, depending on where you are.

✔ If you forget to set the time zone and you end up hopping around the world, your events are set according to the time zone in which they were created, not the local time.

✔ Use the Repetition item to create repeating events, such as weekly or monthly meetings, anniversaries, and birthdays.

✔ Reminders can be set so that the tablet alerts you before an event takes place. The alert can show up as a notification icon (shown in the margin), or it can come in the form of a new Gmail notice (which has its own alert). Pull down the notifications and choose the calendar alert. You can then peruse pending events.

It's an eBook Reader

Your Nexus 7 comes with Google's own eBook reader app. It has the clever name Play Books, and it can be found on the Favorites bar as well as on the All Apps screen.

✔ The Play Books app may come preinstalled with some free books for you to try. Or if you've already purchased Google books, you'll find them waiting in the app. If not, getting free books is easy, as described in this section.

✔ Because the Play Books app is from Google, it uses the Google Play Store as your online bookstore. See Chapter 12 for more information about the Google Play Store.

Using the Play Books app

Begin your reading experience by opening the Play Books app. If you're prompted to turn on synchronization, touch the Turn On Sync button.

The Play Books app organizes the books into a library and displays them for reading, similar to the way they're shown in Figure 11-5. The library lists any titles you've obtained for your Google Books account. Or when you're returning to the Play Books app after a break, you see the current page of the eBook you were last reading.

Scroll through the library by swiping the screen left or right. To begin reading, touch a book to open it. The next section covers how to read a book using the Play Books app.

✔ If you don't see a book in the library, touch the Menu icon button and choose the Refresh command.

✔ To ensure that your reading material is always available, touch the Menu icon button and choose the Make Available Offline command. That way, the Nexus 7 doesn't have to access the Internet in order to synchronize and download books from the library. I choose this command specifically before I leave on a trip where an Internet signal may not be available (such as in an airplane).

- To remove a book from the library, long-press the cover and choose the Remove from My Library command. There's no confirmation: The book is instantly removed.

- Synchronization allows you to keep copies of your Google Books on all your Android devices as well as on the `http://books.google.com` website.

Buy more books.

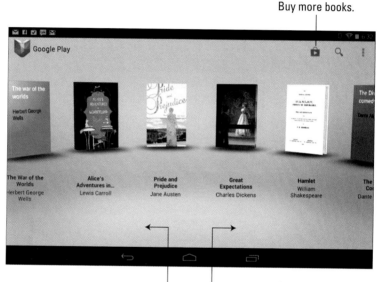

Scroll library left or right.

Figure 11-5: The Play Books library.

Reading an eBook

The eBook experience on the Nexus 7 should be familiar to you, especially if you're reading this text in a "real" book. The entire page-turning-and-reading operation works the same. The only major difference is that you can read a physical book without batteries and in direct sunlight, but I won't dwell on that.

Touch a book in the Play Books app library to open it. If you've opened the book previously, you're returned to the page you last read. Otherwise, the first page you see is the book's first page.

Figure 11-6 illustrates the basic book-reading operation in the Play Books app. You turn pages by swiping left or right, but probably mostly left. You can also turn pages by touching the far left or right side of the screen.

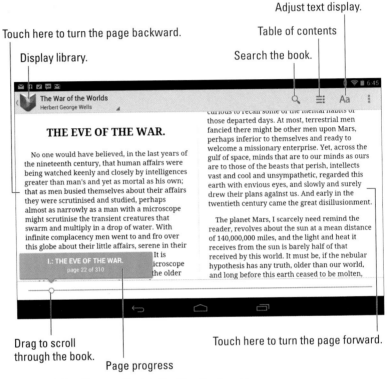

Adjust text display.

Touch here to turn the page backward.   Table of contents

Display library.   Search the book.

Drag to scroll
through the book.   Touch here to turn the page forward.

Page progress

Figure 11-6: Reading an eBook in the Play Books app.

The Play Books app also works in a vertical orientation, though when you turn the tablet that way, only one page is shown at a time.

- ✒ If the onscreen controls (refer to Figure 11-6) disappear, touch the screen to see them again.

- ✒ The Aa button is used to adjust the display. Touching this button displays a palette of options for adjusting the text on the screen and the brightness.

- ✒ To return to the library, touch the Play Books app button in the upper-left corner of the screen or touch the Back icon button.

It's Google Now

The Nexus 7 does dictation just fine. See Chapter 3 for details. But does it understand you? Does it get your meaning? And would you find such a thing extremely helpful or downright creepy?

Don't worry! Your tablet harbors no insidious intelligence, and the Robot Revolution is still years away. Until then, you can use the Nexus 7's listening abilities to enjoy a feature called Google Now. It's not quite like having your own personal Jeeves, but it's on its way.

Summoning Google Now

Abundant opportunities exist for bidding forth Google Now. Figure 11-7 shows the variety.

The most immediate way to summon Google Now is to simply swipe your finger upward from the Home button at the bottom of the screen. Google Now starts instantly.

Figure 11-7: Activating Google Now.

You can also touch the Google bar, found at the top of any Home screen. Touching the bar not only brings forward Google Now but also pops up the onscreen keyboard. Better than that, touch the Microphone button atop the Home screen to activate Google Now in voice input mode.

The main Google Now screen is shown in Figure 11-8. Below the search text box, you'll find cards. The variety and number of cards depend on how often you use Google Now. The more the app learns about you, the more cards appear.

Search for something.

Ask a question.

See sample cards.

Other cards can go here.

Figure 11-8: Google Now is ready for business. Or play.

You can use Google Now to search the Internet, just as you would use Google's main web page. More interesting than that, you can ask Google Now questions, and it responds accordingly. See the next section.

✔ The most boring way to summon Google Now is to visit the All Apps screen and start the Google app. Yes, it's called Google, and not Google Now.

✔ You cannot manually add cards to the Google Now screen. The only way to get more cards to show up is to use Google Now.

Barking various orders

You could be boring and type something at the prompt in the Google Now app. Yawn. Or be like me and just "Google." Say it out loud. Any time you see the Google Now app, as shown in Figure 11-8, the Nexus 7 is listening to you. Utter the word *Google,* and the tablet enters voice input mode.

When saying "Google" doesn't work, such as when you're intoxicated, touch the Microphone button.

You can speak simple search terms, such as "Find me pictures of Megan Fox." The Nexus 7 interprets that text as input, and then it displays the results on the screen. That's interesting, but Google Now is capable of much more.

Here are some sample phrases you can try asking Google Now. They give you an idea of what the app is truly capable of doing:

✔ What's the weather like in Vancouver, British Columbia?

✔ Will it rain tomorrow?

✔ What time is it in Frankfurt, Germany?

✔ How many euros equals $25?

✔ How many liters equals 17 gallons?

✔ What is 103 divided by 6?

✔ How can I get to Disneyland?

✔ Where is the nearest Canadian restaurant?

✔ What was the closing price of Google's stock yesterday?

✔ What's the score of the Lakers–Celtics game?

✔ What is the answer to life, the universe, and everything?

For most of these questions, if not all of them, Google Now responds with a card as well as a verbal reply. When a verbal reply isn't available, you see Google search results displayed at the bottom of the screen.

The more questions you ask, and the more you use Google Now, the more cards appear with the answers on them already available for you.

To find a contact using Google Now, utter the contact's name. When the results appear, touch the Tablet button found at the bottom of the screen.

It's a Photo Album

Some people hang their pictures on the wall. Some put pictures on a piano, or maybe on a mantle. In the digital realm, pictures are stored electronically, compressed and squeezed into a series of ones and zeroes that mean nothing unless you have an app that lets you view those images. On the Nexus 7, this app is the *Gallery*.

Start the Gallery app by choosing its icon from the All Apps screen. When the Gallery app opens, you see pictures organized into piles, or *albums,* as shown in Figure 11-9. The number and variety of albums depend on how you synchronize your tablet with your computer, which apps you use for collecting media, or which photo-sharing services you use on the Internet, such as Picasa.

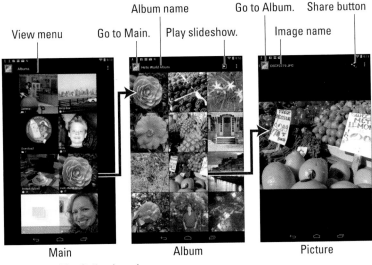

Figure 11-9: The Gallery's main screen.

Touch an album in the Gallery app to display that album's contents; the pictures appear in a grid of thumbnail previews. Swipe the screen left or right to peruse them all.

Touch an individual thumbnail in the album to view the item by itself on the screen. Images appear in full size on the screen, similar to what's shown in Figure 11-9. You can rotate the tablet horizontally (or vertically) to see the image in another orientation.

If any videos are stored in an album, they appear with a large Play button on the screen. Touch that button to play the video. As the video is playing, touch the screen again to see the controls to pause.

You back up from an image or video to an album by touching the Back icon button. Touch the Back icon button again to return to the main Gallery screen.

  ✔ To run a slide show of photos in an album, touch the Slideshow button, shown in Figure 11-9. The slide show starts, displaying one image after another. For videos, only a freeze frame from the video appears. To stop the slide show, touch the screen.

  ✔ The Camera album contains pictures you've shot using the Nexus 7, probably to take your account picture unless you've installed a Camera app.

  ✔ When you view a photo taken by the tablet's camera, the Delete icon button appears at the top of the screen. Touch that button to delete the image; touch the OK button to confirm. You can delete only the images stored in the tablet. To delete Picasa images, you must use Picasa Web on the Internet.

  ✔ The Download album contains images downloaded from the Internet.

  ✔ Albums labeled with the Picasa icon have been synchronized between Picasa Web on the Internet and your Nexus 7.

  ✔ Other albums in the Gallery represent images synchronized between the Nexus 7 and your computer. See Chapter 14 for information on sharing images between the tablet and your computer.

  ✔ Various apps may also create their own albums in the Gallery app.

It's Your Video Entertainment

It's not possible to watch "real" TV on the Nexus 7, but a few apps let you come close. The YouTube app is handy for watching random, meaningless drivel, which I suppose makes it a lot like TV. And then there's the Play Movies app, which lets you buy and rent real movies and TV shows from the Google Play Store. Though you may not be able to pick up and enjoy the local Action News team every day at 5:00 p.m., you're not bereft of video enjoyment on your tablet.

Enjoying YouTube

YouTube is the Internet phenomenon that proves real life is indeed too boring and random for television. Or is it the other way around? Regardless, you can view the latest YouTube videos by using the YouTube app on your Nexus 7.

Search for videos by touching the Search icon button. Type the video name, a topic, or any search terms to locate videos. Zillions of videos are available.

The YouTube app displays suggestions for any channels you're subscribed to, which allows you to follow favorite topics or YouTube content providers.

To view a video, touch its name or icon in the list.

Touch the Full-Screen button to view the video in a larger size. Or just tilt the tablet to the horizontal orientation.

✔ You can instantly share YouTube videos with other Android users, if their phones or tablets sport the Android Beam feature. If so, just touch the back of your Nexus 7 to their mobile device. When prompted, touch the text on the screen to send your friend the video.

✔ Use the YouTube app to view YouTube videos, rather than use the Chrome app to visit the YouTube website.

✔ Because you have a Google account, you also have a YouTube account. I recommend that you log in to your YouTube account when using YouTube on the Nexus 7: Touch the Menu icon button and choose the Sign In command. Log in if you haven't already. Otherwise, you see your account information, your videos, and any video subscriptions.

✔ Not all YouTube videos are available for viewing on mobile devices.

Buying and renting movies

You can use the Google Play Store to not only buy apps and books for your Nexus 7 but also to rent movies. Open the Play Movies app, found on the All Apps screen or accessed from the Favorites bar on the Home screen, to get started.

Renting or purchasing a movie is done at the Play Store, and it works just like purchasing an app. Choose a movie or TV show to rent or buy. Touch the price button, and then choose your method of payment.

Movies and shows rented at the Play Store are available for viewing up to 30 days after you pay the rental fee. After you start the movie, you can pause and watch it again and again during a 24-hour period.

 ✔ Not every film or TV show is available for purchase. Some are rentals only.

 ✔ A Personal Videos category is available in the Play Movies app. It can be used to view any videos stored on the Nexus 7. Because the Nexus 7 lacks a video recording app, that category will probably be empty.

 ✔ One of the best ways to view movies is to connect the tablet to an HDMI monitor or a TV set. This may be possible in the future if a multimedia docking station becomes available for the Nexus 7.

Chapter 12

More Apps at the Play Store

The abilities of your Nexus 7 tablet aren't limited to the paltry assortment of preinstalled apps. No way! A digital cornucopia of apps is available for your tablet — hundreds of thousands, in fact. You have eBooks to read, movies to rent, and music to hoard. All these good things are beheld at the central location called the Google Play Store. Even better, many of these items are available at no cost.

Welcome to the Play Store

People love to shop when they're buying something they want or when they're spending someone else's money. You can go shopping for your Nexus 7, and I'm not talking about buying a docking stand or a combination keyboard cover. I'm talking about apps, music, magazines, movies, TV shows, and books.

Yes! Some people still read books. I find that they're the most handsome people around.

The Google Play Store may sound like the place where you can go to buy outdoor wear for children, but it's really an online place where you go to pick up new goodies for your Nexus 7. You can browse, you can get free stuff, or you can pay. It all happens at the Play Store.

✔ Officially, it's the Google Play Store. It may also be referenced as Google Play. The app, however, is named Play Store.

✔ The Google Play Store was once known as Android Market, and you may still see it referred to as the Market.

✔ This section talks about getting apps for your tablet. For information on getting music, see Chapter 10. Chapter 11 covers renting movies and TV shows. Refer to Chapter 12 for information on books and magazines available at the Play Store.

✔ *App* is short for application. It's a program, or software, you can add to your Nexus 7 to make it do new, wondrous, or useful things.

✔ Because the Nexus 7 uses the Android operating system, it can run nearly all apps written for Android.

✔ The Play Store is available only when the tablet has a Wi-Fi connection. See Chapter 13 for details on configuring the Nexus 7 for Wi-Fi access.

✔ The Play Store app is frequently updated, so its look may change from what you see in this chapter. Updated information on the Google Play Store is available on my website:

```
www.wambooli.com/help/tablets/nexus7
```

Browsing the Google Play Store

You access the Google Play Store by opening the Play Store app, found on the All Apps screen but also on the main Home screen, on the Favorites bar.

After opening the Play Store app, you see the main screen, similar to the one shown on the far left side in Figure 12-1. You can browse for apps, games, books, or movie rentals.

Touch a top-level item to view more details. You can swipe the screen left or right to see different categories, featured items, and best-sellers. Scroll down to peruse the entire list.

After choosing an individual item, you see a screen detailing the specifics, as shown on the far right side in Figure 12-1. Scroll down to glean more information.

When you have an idea of what you want, such as an app's name or even what it does, searching works fastest: Touch the Search button at the top of the Play Store screen. (See Figure 12-1.) Type all or part of the app's name or perhaps a description.

My Apps button   Apps button   Scroll categories.   Share app.

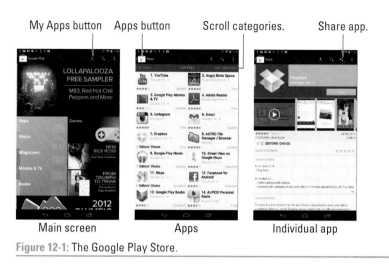

Main screen   Apps   Individual app

Figure 12-1: The Google Play Store.

Return to the previous screen by touching the App button in the upper-left corner of the screen.

✔ The first time you enter the Google Play Store, you have to accept the terms of service; touch the Accept button.

✔ You can be assured that all apps that appear in the Google Play Store can be used with the Nexus 7. There's no way to download or buy something that's incompatible with your tablet.

✔ Pay attention to an app's ratings. Ratings are added by people who use the apps — people like you and me. Having more stars is better. You can see additional information, including individual user reviews, by choosing the app.

✔ Another good indicator of an app's success is how many times it's been downloaded. Some apps have been downloaded over 10 million times. That's a good sign.

✔ In addition to getting apps, you can download widgets for the Home screen as well as wallpapers for the Nexus 7. Just search the Play Store for *widget* or *live wallpaper.*

✔ See Chapter 16 for more information on widgets and live wallpapers.

Obtaining an app

After you locate an app you want, the next step is to download it, by copying it from the Google Play Store on the Internet into your Nexus 7. The app is then installed automatically, building up your collection of apps and expanding what the tablet can do.

Good news: Most apps are available for free. Better news: Even the apps you pay for don't cost dearly. In fact, it seems odd to sit and stew over whether paying 99 cents for a game is "worth it."

I recommend that you download a free app first, to familiarize yourself with the process. Then try your hand at a paid app.

Free or not, the process of obtaining an app works pretty much the same. Follow these steps:

1. **Open the Play Store app.**

2. **Find the app you want and open its description.**

   The app's description screen looks similar to the one shown on the far right side in Figure 12-1.

   The difference between a free app and a paid app is the blue button you use to obtain the app. For a free app, the button says Install. For a paid app, the button shows the app's price.

   You may find three other buttons by an app: Open, Update, and Uninstall. The Open button opens an app that's already installed on your Nexus 7; the Update button updates an already installed app; and the Uninstall button removes an already installed app. See the later sections "Updating an app" and "Removing downloaded apps" for more information on using the Update and Uninstall buttons.

3. **Touch the Install button to get a free app; for a paid app, touch the button with the price on it.**

   Don't fret! You're not buying anything yet.

   You see a screen describing the app's permissions. The list isn't a warning, and it doesn't mean anything bad. It's just that the Play Store is telling you which of your tablet's features the app uses.

4. **For a paid app, choose your credit card.**

   The credit card information is at the top of the Purchase & Allow Access window, on the right. The card must be on file with Google Checkout. If you don't yet have a card on file, choose the option Add Card, and then fill in the fields on the Credit Card screen to add your payment method to Google Checkout.

   If you have any Google Credit, choose your Google Play balance from the credit card list.

5. **Touch the Accept & Download button for a free app; touch the Accept & Buy button for a paid app.**

   For a paid app, you may have to place a blue check mark by the item I Agree to the Payments for Google Play. Only after you do this does the Accept & Buy button become available.

   If you chicken out, touch the Back navigation button. Otherwise, the Downloading notification appears atop the screen as the app is downloaded. You're free to do other things on your Nexus 7 while the app is downloaded and installed.

6. **Touch the Open button to run the app.**

   Or if you were doing something else while the app was downloading and installing, choose the Successfully Installed notification, as shown in the margin. The notification features the app's name with the text *Successfully Installed* beneath it.

At this point, what happens next depends on the app you've downloaded. For example, you may have to agree to a license agreement. If so, touch the I Agree button. Additional setup may involve setting your location, signing in to an account, or creating a profile, for example.

After you complete the initial app setup, or if no setup is necessary, you can start using the app.

➤ Apps you download are added to the All Apps screen, made available like any other app on your tablet.

➤ Some apps may install shortcut icons on the Home screen after they're installed. See Chapter 16 for information on removing the icon from the Home screen, if that is your desire.

➤ For a paid app, you'll receive an e-mail message from the Google Play Store, confirming your purchase. The message contains a link you can click to review the refund policy in case you change your mind on the purchase.

➤ Be quick on that refund: Some apps allow you only 15 minutes to get your money back. You know when the time limit is up because the Refund button on the app's description screen changes its name to Uninstall.

Never buy an app twice

Any apps you've already purchased in the Google Play Store — say, for an Android phone or another mobile device — are available for download to your Nexus 7 at no charge. Simply find the app and touch the Install button.

You can review any already purchased apps in the Play Store: Touch the My Apps button from the top of the screen. In the All category, apps you've already purchased at the Google Play Store appear next to the text *Purchased.* Choose that item to reinstall the paid app.

✔ Peruse the list of services that an app uses (in Step 3) to look for anything unusual or out of line with the app's purpose. For example, an alarm clock app that uses your Contacts list and the text messaging service is a red flag, especially if it's your understanding that the app doesn't need to text-message any of your contacts.

✔ Also see the section "Removing downloaded apps," later in this chapter.

✔ Chapter 20 lists some Android apps that I recommend, all of which are free.

Installing apps from your computer

You don't ever need to use the Nexus 7 to install apps. Using a computer, you can visit the Google Play website, choose software, and have the app installed remotely. It's kind of cool, yet kind of scary. Here's how it works:

1. **Use your computer's web browser to visit the Google Play store on the Internet.**

   The address is `https://play.google.com/store`.

   Bookmark this site in your computer's web browser.

2. **If necessary, click the Sign In link to log in to your Google account.**

   Use the same Google account that you used when setting up your Nexus 7. You need to have access to that account so that Google can remotely update your various Android devices.

3. **Browse for something.**

   You can hunt down apps, books, music — the whole gamut. It works just like browsing the Play Store on your tablet.

4. **After clicking the proper button to obtain the item, choose your Nexus 7 from the Send To menu.**

   The Send To menu lists all your Android devices, or at least those compatible with what you're getting.

   The Nexus 7 tablet may be listed as Asus Nexus 7. Asus is the hardware manufacturer.

5. **For a free app, click the Install button; for a paid app, click the Continue button.**

   If you're getting a free app, installation proceeds. Otherwise, for a paid app, you choose your payment source, such as a credit card, and then click the Buy button.

As if by magic, the app is installed on your Nexus 7 — even though you used a computer to do it.

You probably won't use the Internet on your computer to install most of the software on your tablet. However, it's a great trick to know, especially when you're using the computer and discover some new goodies you may desire for the Nexus 7. In that case, you can remotely install the app, music, book, or whatever. It's handy.

App Management

The Play Store app is not only where you buy apps — it's also used for performing app management. This task includes reviewing apps you've downloaded, updating apps, organizing apps, and removing apps that you no longer want or that you severely hate.

Reviewing your apps

To peruse the apps you've downloaded from the Google Play Store, follow these steps:

1. **Start the Play Store app.**

2. **Touch the My Apps button, found at the top of the screen.**

   Refer to Figure 12-1 for the button's location. It looks similar to the Downloading notification.

3. **Peruse your apps.**

You see two categories for your Play Store apps: Installed and All, as shown in Figure 12-2. Installed apps are found on your tablet; the All apps category includes apps that you have downloaded but that may not be installed. Swipe the screen left or right to switch between categories.

Apps in need of an update   Update button

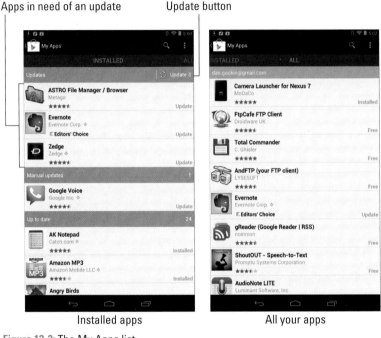

Installed apps   All your apps

Figure 12-2: The My Apps list.

In Figure 12-2, you see three apps in need of an update. One app, Google Voice, needs a manual update. The rest of the apps, starting at the bottom of the screen, are installed and up-to-date.

The All Your Apps screen lists any app you've ever installed on any Android device, even if it's not installed on the Nexus 7. Apps flagged as Installed are, in fact, installed on the tablet. Apps listed as Free or Purchased aren't installed, but can be installed by simply touching their icons.

See the later section "Updating an app" on how the update process works.

Sharing an app

When you love an app so much that you just can't contain your glee, feel free to share the app with your friends. You can easily share a link to the app in the Google Play Store by obeying these steps:

1. **In the Google Play Store, choose the app to share.**

   You can choose any app, but you need to be at the app's details screen, the one with the Free or price button.

 2. **Touch the Share button.**

   A menu appears, listing various apps and methods for sharing the app's Play Store link with your pals.

3. **Choose a sharing method.**

   For example, choose Gmail to send a link to the app in an e-mail message.

4. **Use the chosen app to send the link.**

   What happens next depends on which sharing method you've chosen.

The result of these steps is that your friend receives a link. The person can touch the link on their Android device and be whisked instantly to the Google Play Store, where they can easily install the app.

Methods for using the various items on the Share menu are found throughout this book.

Updating an app

The Play Store notifies you of new versions of your apps. Whenever a new version is available, you see it flagged for updating, as shown in Figure 12-2. Updating the app to get the latest version is cinchy.

Some apps are updated automatically; there's no need for you to do anything. Other apps (refer to Figure 12-2) must be updated individually. You can update a group of apps by touching the Update button, as illustrated in Figure 12-2. For manual updates, choose the item in the list, and then touch the Update button.

To make updating easier, you can place a blue check mark by the item Allow Automatic Updating. Refer to Figure 12-2 for that check box's location.

The updating process often involves downloading and installing a new version of the app. That's perfectly fine; your settings and options aren't changed by the update process.

Even though automatic updating may be configured for some apps, they still require a manual update. Don't ask me why, because I'd just make up a reason.

Removing downloaded apps

I can think of a few reasons to remove an app. It's with eager relish that I remove apps that don't work or somehow annoy me. It's also perfectly okay to remove redundant apps, such as when you're trying to find a decent music-listening app and you end up with a dozen or so that you never use.

Whatever the reason, remove an app by following these directions:

1. **Start the Play Store app.**

2. **Touch the My Apps icon button at the top of the screen.**

   The My Apps icon button looks like the Downloading notification.

3. **In the Installed list, touch the app that offends you.**

4. **Touch the Uninstall button.**

5. **Touch the OK button to confirm.**

   The app is removed.

The app continues to appear on the All list, on the My Apps screen, even after it's been removed. After all, you downloaded it once. That doesn't mean that the app is still installed.

- ✓ In most cases, if you uninstall a paid app right away, your credit card or account is fully refunded. The definition of "right away" depends on the app and is stated on the app's description screen. It can be anywhere from 15 minutes to 24 hours.

- ✓ Removing an app frees a modicum of storage inside the tablet. Just a modicum.

✔ You can always reinstall paid apps that you've uninstalled. You aren't charged twice for doing so.

✔ Some apps are preinstalled on your tablet or are part of the Android operating system. They cannot be removed. I'm sure there's probably a technical way to uninstall these apps, but seriously: Just don't use the apps if you can't remove them.

Part IV
Nuts and Bolts

The 5th Wave   By Rich Tennant

"Frankly, the idea of an entirely wireless future scares me to death."

In this part . . .

Some of the things you do with your Nexus 7 have more to do with settings and adjustments than with being productive, connected, entertained, or anything else the tablet does. These activities lack the glamour of video chat or the thrill of playing a video game. Yet they're required tasks, things you'll do from time to time, and good stuff to know. Though none of this useful information may end up on the side of the box, or included in the Nexus 7 marketing materials, it's found in this part of the book.

Chapter 13

To Be Wireless

*T*o be wireless, or not to be wireless, that is the question: Whether 'tis nobler to be free and unbound by the electric tethers of science, or to be tied by those duty-bound wires, constricted and still.

Yeah, if it were me, I'd choose the wireless life. There's a charm to being portable, light, and free. The battery in the Nexus 7 keeps you away from the power socket for hours. The Wi-Fi networking keeps you unchained from the Internet. And Bluetooth lets the tablet sport a variety of peripherals, nary a wire in sight. If it's wireless, it's covered in this chapter.

Wi-Fi? Why Not!

You know that wireless networking has hit the big-time when you see people asking Santa Claus for a wireless router at Christmas. Such a thing would have been unheard of years ago because routers were used primarily for woodworking back then.

The primary reason for wireless networking on the Nexus 7 is to connect to the Internet. For exchanging and synchronizing files, refer to Chapter 14.

Understanding Wi-Fi

The Nexus 7 uses the same Wi-Fi networking standards as wireless Internet devices, such as laptop computers. So as long as Wi-Fi networking is set up in your home or office, or in the lobby at your proctologist, it's the same.

To make Wi-Fi work on the Nexus 7 requires two steps. First, you must activate Wi-Fi, by turning on the tablet's wireless radio. The second step is connecting to a specific wireless network. It's this network that gives the tablet access to the Internet.

Wi-Fi stands for *wireless fidelity*. It's also known by various famous numbers, including 802.11g and 802.11n.

Activating and deactivating Wi-Fi

Follow these carefully written directions to activate Wi-Fi networking on your Nexus 7:

1. **Touch the All Apps button.**

2. **Open the Settings app.**

3. **Ensure that the button by Wi-Fi is in the ON position.**

    If not, touch the button. It changes from OFF to ON and turns blue.

If your tablet has already been configured to connect to an available wireless network, it's connected automatically. Otherwise, you have to choose, and connect to, an available network, which is covered in the next section.

To turn off Wi-Fi, repeat the steps in this section. Turning off Wi-Fi disconnects the tablet from any wireless networks.

It's perfectly okay to keep the tablet's Wi-Fi on all the time. It drains the battery, but you need that Internet access to get the most from your Nexus 7.

Connecting to a Wi-Fi network

After you've activated the Nexus 7's Wi-Fi radio, you can connect to an available wireless network. You've probably already configured the tablet for your home or office network, as discussed in Chapter 1. When you're out and about and you need to connect to another network, heed these steps:

1. **Touch the All Apps button on the Home screen.**

2. **Open the Settings app.**

3. **Choose Wi-Fi.**

4. **If you're connecting to a WPS wireless router, touch the WPS button on the screen, and then press the WPS button on the wireless router.**

   The WPS button is shown in Figure 13-1. A similar icon appears on the wireless router. After being prompted by the tablet, touch the WPS button on the wireless router to connect the devices. That's it. You're done.

WPS button

Available Wi-Fi networks

Wi-Fi is on.   Wi-Fi connected

                Manually connect.

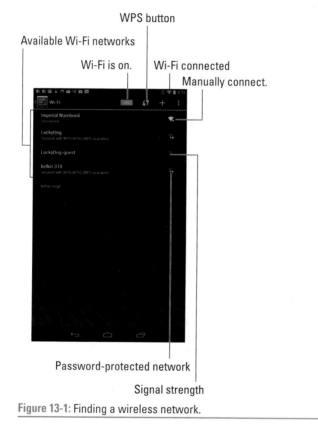

Password-protected network

Signal strength

Figure 13-1: Finding a wireless network.

   If you don't have a WPS router, continue with Step 5:

5. **Choose a wireless network from the list.**

   A list of available Wi-Fi networks appears on the screen, as shown in Figure 13-1. When no wireless networks are listed, you're sort of out of luck regarding wireless access from your current location.

   In Figure 13-1, I chose the Imperial Wambooli network, which is my office network.

6. If prompted, type the network password.

Touch the Show Password check box so that you can see what you're typing. Some of those network passwords can be *long*.

7. Touch the Connect button.

You should be immediately connected to the network. If not, try the password again.

When the Nexus 7 is connected to a wireless network, you see the Wi-Fi Connected status icon. (Refer to Figure 13-1.) This icon indicates that the tablet's Wi-Fi is on, connected, and communicating with a Wi-Fi network.

Some wireless networks don't broadcast their names, which adds security but also makes connecting more difficult. In those cases, touch the Manually Connect button (refer to Figure 13-1) to manually add the network. You need to type the network name, or *SSID*, and choose the type of security. You also need the password if one is used. You can obtain this information from the girl with the pink hair who sold you coffee or from whoever is in charge of the wireless network at your location.

✓ Not every wireless network has a password.

✓ Some public networks are open to anyone, but you have to use the Chrome app to find a login web page that lets you access the network: Simply browse to any page on the Internet, and the login web page shows up.

✓ The Nexus 7 automatically remembers every Wi-Fi network it has ever been connected to and automatically reconnects upon finding the same network again.

✓ To disconnect from a Wi-Fi network, simply turn off Wi-Fi. See the preceding section.

✓ A Wi-Fi network's broadcast signal goes only so far. My advice is to use Wi-Fi whenever you plan to remain in one location for a while. If you wander away, your tablet loses the signal and is disconnected.

The Bluetooth Experience

Computer nerds have long had the desire to connect high-tech gizmos to one another. The Bluetooth standard was developed to sate this desire in a wireless way. Though Bluetooth is wireless *communication,* it's not the same as wireless networking. It's more about connecting peripheral devices, such as keyboards, mice, printers, headphones, and other gear. It all happens in a wireless way, as described in this section.

Understanding Bluetooth

Bluetooth is used to connect two gizmos. One would be your Nexus 7; the other, some type of peripheral. Here's an overview of how the operation works:

1. **Turn on the Bluetooth wireless radio on both gizmos.**

   It takes two Bluetooth gizmos to tango — the peripheral and the main device, such as the Nexus 7.

2. **Make the gizmo you're trying to connect to discoverable.**

   By making a device *discoverable,* you're telling it to send a signal to other Bluetooth devices, saying, "Here I am!"

3. **On the Nexus 7, choose the peripheral from the list of Bluetooth devices.**

   This action is known as *pairing* the devices.

4. **Optionally, confirm the connection on the peripheral device.**

   For example, you may be asked to input a code or press a button.

5. **Use the device.**

   What you can do with the device depends on what it's designed to do.

When you're done using the device, you simply turn it off. Because the Bluetooth peripheral is paired with the Nexus 7, it's automatically reconnected the next time you turn it on (that is, if you have Bluetooth activated on the tablet).

 Bluetooth devices are marked with the Bluetooth icon, shown in the margin. It's your assurance that the peripheral can work with other Bluetooth devices.

 Bluetooth was developed as a wireless version of the old RS-232 standard, the serial port on early personal computers. Essentially, Bluetooth is wireless RS-232, and the variety of devices you can connect to and the things you can do with Bluetooth are similar to what you could do with the old serial port standard.

Activating Bluetooth

To make the Bluetooth connection, you turn on the Nexus 7's Bluetooth radio. Obey these directions:

1. **Touch the All Apps button on the Home screen.**

2. **Open the Settings icon.**

3. **Ensure that the button next to the Bluetooth item is set to ON.**

   If not, touch that button, and the gray OFF button turns into the blue ON button.

 When Bluetooth is on, the Bluetooth status icon appears, as shown in the margin.

To turn off Bluetooth, repeat the steps in this section: Touch the ON button to reset it to OFF in Step 3.

 See Chapter 16 for information on installing the Power Control widget. Using this widget you can quickly turn Bluetooth on or off directly from the Home screen.

Pairing with a Bluetooth device

To make the Bluetooth connection between the Nexus 7 and a Bluetooth peripheral, follow these steps:

1. **Ensure that Bluetooth is on.**

   Refer to the preceding section.

2. **Turn on the Bluetooth gizmo or ensure that its Bluetooth radio is on.**

   Some Bluetooth devices have separate power and Bluetooth switches.

3. **On the Nexus 7, touch the All Apps button on the Home screen and open the Settings app.**

4. **Choose Bluetooth.**

   You see the Bluetooth screen. Any paired devices appear in the list, as shown in Figure 13-2. If any other Bluetooth devices are available for pairing, they show up as well, but normally you have to either scan for those devices or make them discoverable.

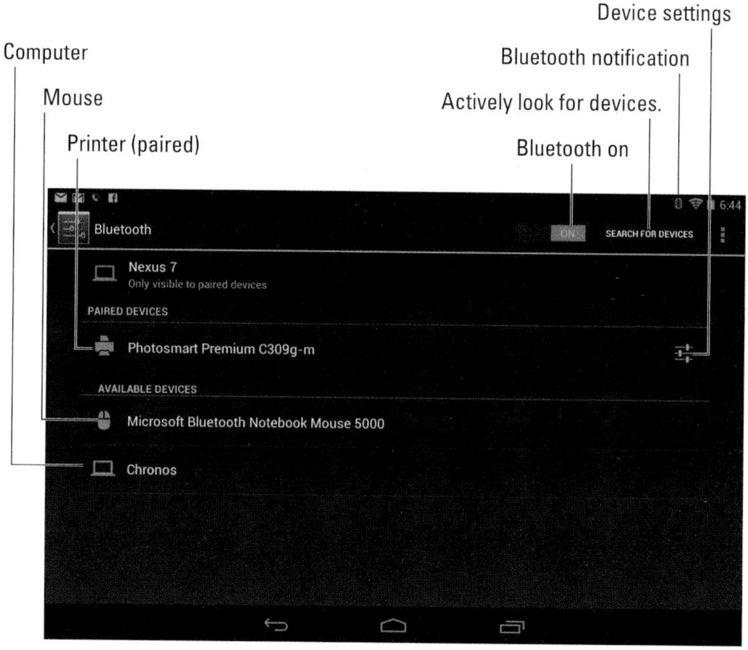

Device settings

Computer   Bluetooth notification

Mouse   Actively look for devices.

Printer (paired)   Bluetooth on

Figure 13-2: Finding Bluetooth gizmos.

5. **If the other device has an option to become visible, select it.**

For example, some Bluetooth gizmos have a tiny button to press that makes the device visible to other Bluetooth gizmos.

The device should appear on the Bluetooth screen, as shown in Figure 13-2. If not, touch the Search For Devices button, as illustrated in the figure.

6. **Choose the device.**

7. **If necessary, input the device's passcode, or otherwise acknowledge the connection.**

Not every device has a passcode. If prompted, acknowledge the passcode on either the Nexus 7 or the other device.

After you acknowledge the passcode (or not), the Bluetooth gizmo and your Nexus 7 are connected and communicating. You can begin using the device.

Connected devices appear in the Bluetooth Settings window, at the bottom, under the heading Paired Devices. In Figure 13-2, a paired printer shows up.

To break the connection, you can either turn off the gizmo or disable the Bluetooth radio on your Nexus 7. Because the devices are paired, when you turn on Bluetooth and reactivate the device, the connection is instantly reestablished.

✒ How you use the device depends on what it does. For example, a Bluetooth keyboard can be used for text input, a computer using Bluetooth can be accessed for sharing files, and a printer can be used for printing documents or pictures, which is covered in the next section.

✒ See Chapter 14 for information on using Bluetooth to transfer files between the Nexus 7 and a computer.

✒ You can unpair a device by touching its settings button, found on the Bluetooth screen. (Refer to Figure 13-2.) Choose the Unpair command to break the Bluetooth connection and stop using the device.

✒ Unpair devices that you don't plan to use again. Otherwise, simply turn off the Bluetooth device when you're done.

Printing to a Bluetooth printer

After your Nexus 7 is connected, or paired, with a Bluetooth printer, you can use the device to print from a variety of apps. The secret is to find and use the Share button or command, choose Bluetooth, and then select your printer. Of course, here are some more detailed steps:

1. **View the document, web page, or image you want to print.**

   You can print from the Chrome app, Gallery app, or Maps app, or from a number of apps you can install on your Nexus 7.

2. **Choose the Share command.**

   If a Share button isn't visible in the app, touch the Menu icon button to look for the Share command.

3. **Choose Bluetooth from the menu.**

4. **Choose your Bluetooth printer from the list of items on the Bluetooth Device Chooser screen.**

   In the Gallery app, touch the Bluetooth button when the image is displayed to see the Bluetooth Device Chooser screen.

5. **If a prompt appears on the printer, confirm that the Nexus 7 is printing a document.**

The document is uploaded (sent from the tablet to the printer), and then it prints. You can view the upload status by checking the notifications in the lower-right corner of the screen.

Not everything on your Nexus 7 can be printed on a Bluetooth printer. When you can't find the Share command or the Bluetooth item isn't available on the Share menu, you can't print using Bluetooth.

- ↙ Bluetooth printers sport the Bluetooth logo somewhere.
- ↙ To print from the Maps app, view a location's information, and choose the command Share This Location. Choose Bluetooth.

Android Beam It to Me

The Nexus 7 tablet features an NFC radio, where *NFC* stands for Near Field Communications and *radio* is a type of vegetable.

NFC allows your tablet to communicate with other NFC devices, which allows for the quick transfer of information. The technology is called Android Beam.

Turning on NFC

The NFC radio should already be activated for your Nexus 7. If not, or to confirm, follow these steps:

1. **At the Home screen, touch the All Apps button.**
2. **Choose the Settings icon to open the Settings app.**
3. **Touch the More command found beneath the Wireless & Networks heading.**
4. **Ensure that a blue check mark appears by the NFC item.**

   If it doesn't, touch the box to add a blue check mark.
5. **Touch the Home button to quit the Settings app.**

With NFC activated, you can use your tablet to communicate with other NFC devices. They include other tablets and smartphones, as well as payment systems for various merchants.

To disable NFC, repeat these steps, but in Step 4 remove the blue check mark.

Activating the NFC radio doesn't noticeably impact battery life on your tablet. Feel free to leave it on all the time.

Using Android Beam

The way your Nexus 7 puts NFC communications to work is through the *Android Beam* feature. It works when you simply touch your tablet to another NFC device, such as another Nexus 7 or a smartphone, like the Samsung Galaxy S III.

When the two Android Beam devices touch — usually back-to-back — you see a prompt appear on the screen: Touch to Beam. Touch the screen, and the item you're viewing is immediately sent to the other device. That's pretty much it.

- Both devices present the Touch to Beam prompt when they get close. If the other person touches his screen at the same time you do, information is swapped between the devices.

- On the Nexus 7, you can use Android Beam to swap contacts, web pages, map locations, pictures, and lots of other things. Generally speaking, if the app features the Share button, you can probably use Android Beam.

- The NFC field on the Nexus 7 is found on the upper back of the device.

- Android Beam can be used to make payments without having to use a credit card, by using a feature called Google Wallet. Lamentably, the Wallet app included on the Nexus 7 seems to work only with one specific credit card. If you don't have that card, you're urged to sign up for it — no other cards appeared to be accepted at the time this book was published. When other payment methods are available, I'll have more to say about the Wallet app.

Using Jim Beam

Follow these steps to enjoy a bottle of Kentucky straight bourbon whiskey:

1. **Unscrew cap.**

2. **Pour.**

3. **Enjoy.**

It isn't truly necessary to pour the whiskey into another container for consumption, though many users find a glass, mug, or red Solo cup useful.

Alcohol and social networking do not mix.

Chapter 14

Connect and Share

The Nexus 7 is adept at communicating wirelessly. It can connect to the Internet using a Wi-Fi connection, it can use wireless peripherals with Bluetooth, it can exchange information using Android Beam. Beyond that, you can use the USB cable to connect your tablet to another gizmo. No, you cannot use the USB cable to connect the Nexus 7 to the couch, or the toaster, or a nuclear weapon. You can, however, use the USB cable to connect the Nexus 7 to a computer. This chapter describes all the wonderful things that can happen after you make that connection.

The USB Connection

The most direct way to connect a Nexus 7 to a computer is by using a wire — specifically, the wire nestled cozily in the heart of a USB cable. You can do lots of things after making the USB connection. It all starts with connecting the cable.

Connecting the Nexus 7 to your computer

The USB connection between the Nexus 7 and your computer works fastest when the devices are physically connected. You make this connection happen by using the USB cable that comes with the tablet. Like nearly every computer cable in the Third Dimension, the USB cable has two ends:

✓ The A end of the USB cable plugs into the computer.

✓ The other end of the cable plugs into the bottom of the Nexus 7.

The connectors are shaped differently and cannot be plugged in either backward or upside down.

After you understand how the cable works, plug the USB cable into one of the computer's USB ports. Then plug the USB cable into the Nexus 7. What happens next is described in the following sections.

✓ Unlike other Android devices, the Nexus 7 does not show a USB connection status icon atop the screen when the connection is made.

✓ By connecting the Nexus 7 to your computer, you are adding, or *mounting*, its internal storage to your computer's storage system. This process allows file transfers to take place.

✓ Even if you don't use the USB cable to communicate with the computer, the Nexus 7's battery charges when it's connected to a computer's USB port — as long as the computer is turned on, of course.

Dealing with the USB connection in Windows

Between the Nexus 7 and your PC, you'll find it's the PC that exhibits the most concern when the two devices are connected. You'll most likely see an AutoPlay dialog box appear when the tablet is first connected. Two different AutoPlay dialog boxes can appear, as shown in Figure 14-1, depending on how the USB connection is configured on the Nexus 7.

The Nexus 7 as media player · · · · · · The Nexus 7 as digital camera

Figure 14-1: The Nexus 7 AutoPlay dialog boxes.

In Windows 7, things work differently. This prompt appears on the screen: Tap to Choose What Happens with This Device. Click or touch the prompt to view suggestions similar to those found in the AutoPlay dialog boxes. (Refer to Figure 14-1.)

Choose an option from the AutoPlay dialog box, or just close the dialog box. Later sections in this chapter explain when to use certain options.

- See the later section "Configuring the USB connection" for information on the difference between MTP and PTP.

- The AutoPlay dialog box may not appear when you connect the Nexus 7 to your PC. It's possible to configure Windows not to display that dialog box, though if you've not messed with the AutoPlay settings, an AutoPlay dialog box shows up.

- Even if the AutoPlay dialog box doesn't appear, you can still access media and files stored on the Nexus 7 from your computer. The later section "Files Back and Forth" has details.

 If you're nerdy, you can open the Nexus 7's icon in the Computer window; press the Win+E keyboard shortcut on your PC to see the Computer window. You'll find the Nexus 7 listed as either a Portable Media Player (MTP) or Digital Camera (PTP) connection. Open the Nexus 7 icon to browse the tablet's internal storage.

Connecting the Nexus 7 to a Mac

You need special software to goad your Nexus 7 and Macintosh into communicating; the Mac doesn't natively recognize the tablet. Download the software from this website:

```
www.android.com/filetransfer
```

Install the software. Run it. From that point on, when you connect the Nexus 7 to the Macintosh, you see a Finder window appear, listing all folders and files found on the Nexus 7. Use the window for file management, as covered later in this chapter.

 The Mac recognizes the Nexus 7 only if the tablet is configured as an MTP device. Refer to the next section to confirm that the tablet is properly configured.

Configuring the USB connection

The difference between the MTP and PTP connections are in how your computer recognizes the Nexus 7. If you've set the USB connection to MTP, the computer is fooled into thinking that the Nexus 7 is a portable media player. For the PTP connection, the PC believes the tablet to be a digital camera.

Determining whether the Nexus 7 uses the MTP or PTP connection is done by following these steps:

1. **At the Home screen, touch the All Apps button.**

2. **Open the Settings app.**

3. **Choose Storage.**

4. **Touch the Menu icon button, and then choose the command USB Computer Connection.**

   The two options are MTP and PTP.

5. **Ensure that there's a check mark by the Media Device (MTP) option.**

6. **Touch the Home navigation button to return to the Home screen.**

I recommend using the MTP connection because it's the most flexible. If you find the Nexus 7 not recognized by your Windows computer, rework these steps and choose the PTP option.

MTP stands for *Media Transfer Protocol*. PTP stands for *Picture Transfer Protocol*. Do not bother memorizing these terms.

Disconnecting the Nexus 7

The process is cinchy: When you're done transferring files, music, or other media between your PC and the tablet, close all programs and folders you have opened on your computer — specifically, those you've used to work with the tablet's storage. Then you can disconnect the USB cable. That's it.

✔ It's a Bad Idea to unplug the tablet while you're transferring information or while a folder window is open on your computer. Doing so can damage the Nexus 7's internal storage, rendering unreadable some of the information that's kept there. To be safe, close those programs and folder windows you've opened before disconnecting.

✔ Unlike other external storage on the Macintosh, there's no need to eject the Nexus 7's storage when you're done accessing it. Simply unplug the tablet. The Mac doesn't get angry when you do so.

Files Back and Forth

The point of making the USB connection between your Nexus 7 and the computer is to exchange files. You can't just wish the files over. Instead, I recommend following the advice in this section, which also covers transferring files using Bluetooth.

A good understanding of basic computer operations is necessary before you attempt file transfers between your computer and the Nexus 7. You need to know how to copy, move, rename, and delete files. It also helps to be familiar with what folders are and how they work. The good news is that you don't need to manually calculate a 64-bit cyclical redundancy check on the data, nor do you need to know what a parity bit is.

Transferring files to the Nexus 7

I can think of plenty of reasons that you would want to copy a file from your computer to the Nexus 7. You can copy over your pictures and videos, music or audio files, or even vCards that help you build contacts for the People app. You can even copy random files when you're on a caffeine high and there's nothing on TV.

Follow these steps to copy a file or two from your computer to the Nexus 7:

1. **Connect the Nexus 7 to the computer by using the USB cable.**

   Specific directions are offered earlier in this chapter.

2. **On a Windows computer, if the AutoPlay dialog box appears, choose the option Open Device to View Files. Otherwise, open the Computer window, and then open the Nexus 7's icon. To access the tablet's files, open the Internal Storage icon.**

   There's no need to mess with anything on a Macintosh — the Nexus 7's folder window opens up, all bright and sun-shiny, on the screen.

   The folder window you see looks like any other folder window. The difference is that the files and folders in this window are stored on the Nexus 7, not on your computer.

3. **Locate the files you want to copy to the Nexus 7.**

   Open the folder that contains the files, or somehow have the file icons visible on the screen.

4. **Drag the file icon from its folder on your computer to the Nexus 7 folder window.**

   If you want to be specific, drag the file to the `download` folder; otherwise, you can place the file in the Nexus 7's root folder. (See Figure 14-2.) Avoid dragging the file into other, specific folders, which would make the file more difficult to locate later.

5. **Close the folder windows, and disconnect the USB cable when you're done.**

   Refer to specific instructions earlier in this chapter.

Drag files to here to
copy to the "root."

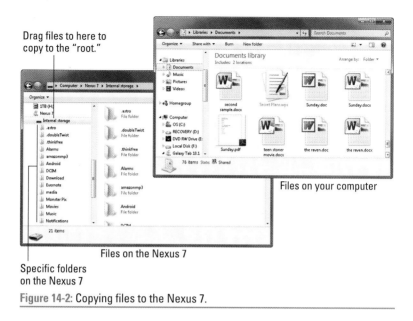

Files on your computer

Files on the Nexus 7

Specific folders
on the Nexus 7

Figure 14-2: Copying files to the Nexus 7.

Any files you've copied are now stored on the Nexus 7. What you
do with them next depends on the reasons you copied the files:
to view pictures, use the Gallery, import vCards, use the Contacts
app, listen to music, or use the Music app, for example.

✔ Copying music to the Nexus 7 is tricky. The tablet doesn't
recognize every music file format, such as the WMA format,
which is popular in Windows. Copy MP3 audio files only if you
want to listen to them on the Nexus 7.

✔ The best way to synchronize music is by using a music
jukebox program on your computer. Lamentably, neither
Windows Media Player nor iTunes behaves well with the
Nexus 7. That situation may change in the future.

✔ My advice is to drag the files you want to copy to the Nexus 7
to your computer's desktop. Make a little pile of them there.
Then you can drag over the lot to "lasso" them as a batch and
drag them over to the tablet's folder.

Copying files to your computer

If you've survived the ordeal of copying files from your computer to the Nexus 7, copying files in the other direction is a cinch: Follow the steps in the preceding section, but in Steps 3 and 4 you're dragging the file icons from the Nexus 7 folder window to your computer.

- Files you've downloaded on the Nexus 7 are stored in the `Download` folder.

- Pictures and videos on the Nexus 7 are stored in the `DCIM/Camera` folder.

- Music on the Nexus 7 is stored in the `Music` folder, organized by artist.

- Quite a few files can be found in the *root folder,* the main folder on the Nexus 7, which you see when the tablet is mounted into your computer's storage system and you open the `Internal Storage` folder.

Chapter 15

On the Road

*L*ast time I checked, the Nexus 7 didn't come with legs. It doesn't even have a rolling tread, like a tank. That would be awesome, and I'm sure that more Real Men would buy a Nexus 7 with a tank tread, but it's not my point: The Nexus 7 is a mobile device. It's wireless. It runs on battery power. You can take the Nexus 7 with you everywhere you go and not draw those peculiar looks you get when you take the washing machine with you.

You Can Take It with You

How far can you go with the Nexus 7? As far as you want. As long as you can carry the tablet with you, it goes where you go. How it functions may change depending on your environment, and you can do a few things to prepare before you go, which are all covered in this section.

Preparing to leave

Unless you're being unexpectedly abducted, you should prepare several things before leaving on a trip with your Nexus 7.

First and most important, of course, is to charge the thing. I plug in my Nexus 7 overnight before I leave the next day. The battery in the tablet is nice and robust, so it should last you your entire journey.

Second, consider loading up on some reading material, music, and a few new apps before you go.

For example, consider getting some eBooks for the road. I prefer to sit and stew over the Play Store's online library before I leave, as opposed to wandering aimlessly in the airport sundry store, trying hard to focus on the good books rather than on the salty snacks. Chapter 11 covers reading eBooks on your Nexus 7.

Picking up some music might be a good idea as well. Visit Chapter 10.

I usually reward myself with a new game before I go on a trip with my tablet. Visit the Play Store to see what's hot or recommended. A good puzzle game can make a nice, long international flight go by a lot quicker.

Going to the airport

I'm not a frequent flier, but I am a nerd. The most amount of junk I've carried with me on a flight is two laptop computers and three cell phones. I know that's not a record, but it's enough to warrant the following list of travel tips, all of which apply to taking the Nexus 7 with you on an extended journey:

- ✔ Take the Nexus 7's AC adapter and USB cable with you. Put them in your carry-on luggage.

- ✔ Many airports feature USB chargers, so you can charge the tablet in an airport, if you need to. Even though you need only the cable to charge, bring along the AC adapter anyway.

- ✔ At the security checkpoint, place your Nexus 7 in a bin by itself or with other electronics.

- ✔ Use the Calendar app to keep track of your flights. The event title serves as the airline and flight number. For the event time, use the take-off and landing schedules. For the location, list the origin and destination airport codes. And in the Description field, put the flight reservation number. If you're using separate calendars (categories), specify the Travel calendar for your flight.

- ✔ See Chapter 11 for more information on the Calendar app.

- ✔ Some airlines feature Android apps that you can use while traveling. At the time this book went to press, American Airlines, Continental, Southwest, United, and a host of other airlines featured apps. You can use the apps to not only keep track of flights but also check in: Eventually, printed tickets will disappear, and you'll merely show your "ticket" on the Nexus 7 screen, which will then be scanned at the gate.

✔ Some of the apps you can use to organize your travel details are similar to, but more sophisticated than, the Calendar app. Visit the Google Play Store, and search for *travel* or *airline* to find a host of apps.

Flying with the Nexus 7

It truly is the most trendy of things to be aloft with the latest mobile gizmo. Like taking a cell phone on a plane, however, you have to follow certain rules. Though the Nexus 7 isn't a cell phone, you still have to heed the flight crew's warnings regarding cell phones and other electronics.

First and foremost, turn off the Nexus 7 when instructed to do so. This direction is given before take-off and landing, so be prepared.

Before take-off, you'll most likely want to put the tablet into Airplane mode. Yep, it's the same Airplane mode you see on a cell phone: The various scary and dangerous wireless radios on the tablet are disabled in this mode. With Airplane mode active, you're free to use the tablet in-flight, and you can rest assured that with Airplane mode active, you face little risk of the Nexus 7 causing the plane's navigational equipment to fail and the entire flight to end as a fireball over Wyoming.

To enter Airplane mode on the Nexus 7, follow these steps just before take-off:

1. **Pull down the Quick Actions shade.**

   You need to pull down starting from the right half of the screen, otherwise you pull down the Notifications shade.

2. **Touch the Airplane Mode box.**

3. **Touch the Back button to hide the Quick Actions shade.**

When the Nexus 7 is in Airplane mode, a special icon appears on the status bar.

And now, for an even faster shortcut: To put the Nexus 7 into Airplane mode, press and hold the Power button and choose the Airplane Mode command.

To exit Airplane mode, repeat the steps in this section.

✔ Officially, the Nexus 7 must be powered off when the plane is taking off or landing. See Chapter 1 for information on turning off the tablet.

✔ You can compose e-mail while the tablet is in Airplane mode. The messages aren't sent until you disable Airplane mode and connect again by using a data network.

✔ Bluetooth wireless is disabled in Airplane mode. Even so:

✔ Many airlines now feature wireless networking onboard, which you can use with the Nexus 7 — if you're willing to pay for the service. Simply activate Wi-Fi on the tablet, per the directions in Chapter 13, and then connect to the in-flight wireless network when it's available.

The Nexus 7 Travels Abroad

You have no worries taking the Wi-Fi Nexus 7 abroad. Because it uses Wi-Fi signals, your biggest issue is simply finding wireless Internet access so that you can use your tablet's communications abilities. Well, that and finding the four-pronged power outlet adapter — the one with two square prongs, one round prong, and one prong that's bent.

✔ The tablet's AC plug can easily plug into a foreign AC adapter, which allows you to charge the tablet in outer Wamboolistan. From personal experience, I can tell you that I charged my tablet nightly while I spent time in France, and it worked like a charm.

✔ You don't need a power converter to charge the tablet. Simply obtain a power adapter, one that lets you plug the charger into the weirdo foreign plug.

✔ Wi-Fi Internet access is nearly universal. As long as your location offers this service, you can connect the tablet and pick up your e-mail, browse the web, or do whatever other Internet activities you desire.

✔ Most foreign hotels I've been to offer free Wi-Fi for their guests. Even when it's available only in the lobby, it works.

✔ Even when you have Wi-Fi, you need Skype Credit to make a phone call. Calls to other Skype users are free, but to phone home to Aunt Olivia who has only a landline, you need Skype Credit. See Chapter 8 for more information on making Skype calls.

Chapter 16

Customize Your Nexus 7

*I*t's entirely possible to own the amazing Nexus 7 for the rest of your life and never even once bother to customize the tablet. It's not only possible, it's sad. That's because there exists great potential to make the device truly your own. You can change so many things, from the way it looks to the way it sounds. The reason isn't simply to change things because you can, but to make the tablet work best for how you use it. After all, it's *your* Nexus 7.

Home Screen Decorating

Lots of interesting doodads can festoon the Nexus 7 Home screen, like bacon bits on a salad. You can set the background, add an icon or a widget, and rearrange everything to your heart's content. Or when your heart isn't content, you choose to make your gall bladder content. Either way, directions and suggestions are offered in this section.

Hanging new wallpaper

The Home screen has two types of backgrounds, or *wallpapers*: traditional and live. A *live* wallpaper is animated. A not-so-live (*traditional*) wallpaper can be any image, such as a picture stored in the Gallery app.

To set a new wallpaper for the Home screen, obey these steps:

1. Long-press any empty part of the Home screen.

The empty part doesn't have a shortcut icon or widget floating on it.

Upon success, you see the Choose Wallpaper From menu.

2. Select a wallpaper type.

Three options are available:

Gallery: Choose a still image from the Gallery app.

Live Wallpapers: Choose an animated or interactive wallpaper from a list.

Wallpapers: Choose a wallpaper from a range of images preinstalled on the Nexus 7.

3. Choose the wallpaper you want from the list.

For the Gallery option, browse the albums to choose an image. Crop the image to select the portion you want included on the Home screen.

For certain live wallpapers, the Settings button may appear. The settings let you customize certain aspects of the interactive wallpaper.

4. Touch the OK or Set Wallpaper button to confirm your selection.

The new wallpaper takes over the Home screen.

Live wallpaper features some form of animation, which can often be interactive. Otherwise, the wallpaper image scrolls slightly as you swipe from one Home screen panel to another.

The Zedge app provides an über-repository of wallpaper images, collected from Android users all over the world. Check out Zedge at the Google Play Store; see Chapter 12.

Adding apps to the Home screen

The first thing I did on my Nexus 7 was to place icons for my most favorite apps on the Home screen. Here's how it works:

1. Touch the All Apps button on the Home screen.

2. Long-press the app icon that you want to add to the Home screen.

After a moment, you see a Home screen panel preview displayed, as shown in Figure 16-1.

Drag here to   Show app's
uninstall the app.   Info screen.

Drag here to move one panel to the left.

Drag the icon to a position on the Home screen.

Icon grid position

Drag here to move one panel to the right.

Figure 16-1: Stick an app on the Home screen.

3. Drag the app to a position on one of the Home screen panels.

4. Position the app where you want it to go and lift your finger.

An outline appears on the Home screen panel preview, showing you where you the icon goes when you lift your finger. Any other icons that are in the way are shuffled around to make room for the new one.

The app hasn't moved: What you see is a copy. You can still find the app on the All Apps screen, but now the app is — more conveniently — available on the Home screen.

✔ Everything on the Home screen is movable. If you don't want an app or widget on the main Home screen panel, move it. See the later section "Moving and removing icons and widgets."

✔ Also see that section if you change your mind somewhere between Steps 3 and 4 in this section. If you don't want the app on the Home screen, drop it there anyway, and then remove it.

✔ Keep your favorite apps, those you use most often, on the Home screen.

✔ Icons on the Home screen are aligned to a grid. You can't stuff more icons on the Home screen than will fit in the grid, so when a Home screen is full of icons (or widgets), use another Home screen panel.

Building app folders

The Nexus 7 has only five home screens, and the grid has only so much room for apps. Especially when you use large widgets, sometimes you just run out of space. Or maybe you have a collection of similar apps, such as games, that you want to organize on the Home screen. A solution you can try is to create an app folder.

An *app folder* is simply a collection of two or more apps, both in the same spot on the Home screen. A sample folder of Google apps is created on the far left end of the Favorites bar. Figure 16-2 shows what folders can look like.

To build a folder, simply drag one app icon over another. To drag an icon, long-press it and keep your finger down. Move that icon over another icon and release your finger. The two icons appear inside a black circle, as shown in Figure 16-2.

Open a folder by touching it. You can then touch an icon to start an app.

✔ Folders are managed just like other icons on the Home screen. You can long-press them to drag them around. They can also be deleted. See the later section "Moving and removing icons and widgets."

✔ Change a folder's name by opening the folder and then long-pressing the name. Type the new name using the onscreen keyboard.

✔ You can add an app icon to a folder by dragging it to the folder when you add that icon to the Home screen.

✔ If you add an app icon by dragging it over an existing icon on the Home screen, you create a folder instantly.

✔ To remove an icon from a folder, open the folder and drag the icon out.

✔ When the second-to-last last icon is dragged out of a folder, the folder is removed. The last icon in the folder then becomes a solitary icon, just like other icons on the Home screen.

✔ Using my nerd calculator, I multiplied five Home screen panels by 36 potential icon spots on each panel. That makes for a total of 180 app icon shortcuts on the Home screen. Add six more on the Favorites bar and you get 186. That's not counting any folders or any space occupied by widgets.

Folder icon   Open folder.

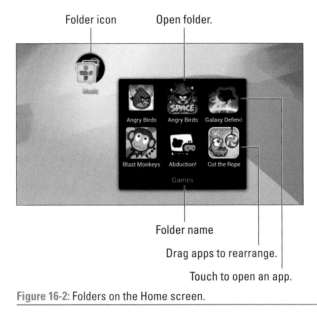

Folder name

Drag apps to rearrange.

Touch to open an app.

Figure 16-2: Folders on the Home screen.

Putting an app on the Favorites bar

Apps stored on the Favorites bar appear on every Home screen. Though you can't replace the All Apps button in the middle of the Favorites bar, all the other icons are up for grabs. You can move those apps off the Favorites bar, combine them into folders, or delete them, as covered elsewhere in this chapter.

Working with icons on the Favorites bar works just like working with any other icons on the Home screen: Long-press an icon and drag it around, keeping your finger on the screen.

To place an icon on the Favorites bar, first move an existing icon off the Favorites bar: Long-press the icon and drag it up to the Home screen. Then you can drag any other icon from the Home screen — or from the All Apps screen — to the Favorites bar.

If you don't first move an existing icon off the Favorites bar and then you try to add another icon on top of it, you create a folder. See the preceding section for information on folders.

Slapping down widgets

A *widget* works like a tiny, interactive or informative window, often providing a gateway into another app on the Nexus 7. Just as you can add apps to the Home screen, you can also add widgets.

The Nexus 7 comes with a smattering of widgets preaffixed to the Home screen, possibly just to show you how they can be used. That includes one massive widget, the My Library widget, appearing on the center Home screen.

You can place even more widgets on the Home screen by following these steps:

1. **Touch the All Apps button on the Home screen.**

2. **Touch the Widgets category atop the screen.**

   Or just scroll the list of apps to the left until you see widgets displayed.

   The widgets appear on the All Apps screen in little preview windows.

3. **Scroll the list to find the widget you want to add.**

   Some widgets, such as the contact widgets, are icon-size. Some are quite large. That's okay — you can resize widgets as covered in the next section.

A great widget to add is the Power Control widget, which contains options for changing popular settings on the Nexus 7, as shown in Figure 16-3.

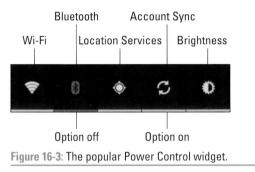

Figure 16-3: The popular Power Control widget.

4. Long-press the widget, and drag it to a Home screen panel.

The widget is plopped on the Home screen.

The variety of available widgets depends on the applications you have installed. Some applications come with widgets, some don't. Some widgets come independently of any application.

✔ The Home screen panel must have room for the widget or else the tablet doesn't let you plop down the widget. Choose another panel, or remove icons or widgets to make room.

✔ To remove a widget, see the later section "Moving and removing icons and widgets."

✔ The Nexus 7 has widgets for contacts, bookmarks, and navigation. On other Android devices, these widgets would be called *shortcuts*. On your tablet, they're widgets.

✔ More widgets are available at the Google Play Store. See Chapter 12. Also, see Chapter 18 for information on Lock screen widgets.

Resizing widgets

Big widgets
Small widgets
Widgets that change size
Wide widgets
Tall widgets
Change before your eyes

Some widgets can change their size, some cannot. To find out which, long-press the widget. If the widget can be resized, you see four dots appear on the edges. (Lift your finger after long-pressing the widget.) The dots are *handles,* which you can drag using your finger to resize the widget.

Some widgets can be resized in only two directions: left-right or up-down.

You can also drag a widget by its corner to resize in two directions at a time.

Touch anywhere on the Home screen when you're done resizing a widget.

Moving and removing icons and widgets

Icons and widgets are fastened to the Home screen by something akin to the same glue they use on sticky notes. You can easily pick up an icon or a widget, move it around, and then restick it. Unlike sticky notes, the icons and widgets never just fall off, or so I'm told.

To move an icon or a widget, long-press it. Eventually, the icon seems to lift and break free, as shown in Figure 16-4.

You can drag a free icon to another position on the Home screen or to another Home screen panel, or you can drag it to the Remove icon that appears at the top of the Home screen, as shown in Figure 16-4.

Widgets and folders can be moved around or deleted in the same manner as icons.

✔ Dragging a Home screen icon or widget to the Remove icon ousts that icon or widget from the Home screen. It doesn't uninstall the app or widget, which is still found on the All Apps screen. In fact, you can always add the icon or widget to the Home screen again, as described earlier in this chapter.

✔ When an icon, a widget, or a folder hovers over the Remove icon, ready to be deleted, its color changes to red.

✔ See Chapter 12 for information on uninstalling applications.

✔ Your clue that an icon or a widget is free and clear to navigate is that the Remove icon appears. (Refer to Figure 16-4.)

Delete icon or widget.

Long-press to "lift" icon.

Figure 16-4: Moving an icon about.

Nexus 7 Security

You can secure your tablet from access by evildoers in a number of ways. The first method of protection is to employ a lock screen, specifically one better than the standard sliding lock that the Nexus 7 uses. The second method is to use data encryption on the tablet's contents. Finally, you can take advantage of the Owner Info text. All these security techniques are covered in this section.

Finding the lock screens

Lock screen security is set on the Choose Screen Lock screen. Here's how to get there:

1. **At the Home screen, touch the All Apps button.**

2. **Open the Settings app.**

3. **Choose Security.**

4. **Choose Screen Lock.**

5. **If a screen lock is already set, you must trace the pattern or type the PIN or password to continue.**

The Choose Lock Screen window lists six types of lock settings:

None: The screen doesn't lock. Even the Unlock-button-and-locking-ring thingy doesn't show up. Choosing this option disables all locks.

Slide: The Nexus 7 simply uses the standard locking screen: Slide the Unlock button to the unlocking ring, as described in Chapter 1.

Face Unlock: Use the front camera on the Nexus 7 to use your adorable face as the unlocking mechanism.

Pattern: To unlock the tablet, you must trace a pattern on the touchscreen.

PIN: The Nexus 7 is unlocked by typing a personal identification number (PIN).

Password: You must type a password to unlock the Nexus 7.

To set or remove a lock, refer to the following sections.

Removing the screen lock

You use the Choose Lock Screen window to not only place a lock on your tablet, but also remove any existing locks.

After visiting the Choose Lock Screen window, as described in the preceding section, you can choose the None option to remove all screen locks. Or to restore the original screen lock, choose the Slide option.

Unlocking the tablet with your face

Don't smash your nose into the Nexus 7! The Face Unlock setting allows you to get access to your Nexus 7 simply by looking at it. Or, well, I suppose that someone could hold up a picture of you to unlock the tablet. Perhaps Google didn't think of that? Anyway, to set the Face Unlock option, follow these steps:

1. **Get to the Choose Screen Lock window.**

   Refer to the earlier section "Finding the lock screens" for specific directions.

2. **Choose Face Unlock.**

   In the directions on the screen that you probably didn't read, it says that Face Unlock is less secure than other forms of locking the phone. But it's fun, so what the heck?

3. **Touch the Set It Up button.**

4. **Hold up the tablet so that it's facing you at eye level — as though you were using the Nexus 7 as a mirror.**

5. **Touch the Continue button.**

6. **Line up your face with the oval dots on the screen, and then hold the tablet steady as the dots change from white to green.**

7. **Upon success, touch the Continue button.**

8. **Choose Pattern or PIN to set a backup lock for those numerous times that Face Unlock fails.**

   Refer to later sections in this chapter for how to set up these types of locks.

9. **After confirming the pattern or PIN lock, touch the OK button.**

   The Face Unlock is now ready for action.

Most of the time, Face Unlock works fine. When it doesn't, you need to use the backup pattern or PIN lock. You also need to use the pattern or PIN whenever you need to change the lock, as discussed in the earlier section "Finding the lock screens."

Creating an unlock pattern

One of the most common ways to lock the Nexus 7 is to apply an *unlock pattern:* The pattern must be traced exactly as it was created to unlock the device and get access to your apps and other features.

1. **Summon the Choose Screen Lock window.**

   Refer to the earlier section "Finding the lock screens."

2. **Choose Pattern.**

   If you've not yet set a pattern lock, you may see a tutorial describing the process. Touch the Next button to skip over the dreary directions.

3. **Trace an unlock pattern.**

   Use Figure 16-5 as your inspiration. You can trace over the dots in any order, but you can trace over a dot only once. The pattern must cover at least four dots.

Continue tracing.

Pattern so far

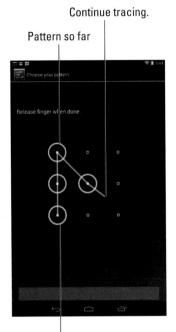

I began the pattern here.

Figure 16-5: Set an unlock pattern.

4. Touch the Continue button.

5. Redraw the pattern.

You need to prove to the doubtful tablet that you know the pattern.

6. Touch the Confirm button.

And the pattern lock is set.

 Ensure that a check mark appears by the option Make Pattern Visible on the Screen Security Window. The check mark ensures that the pattern shows up. For even more security, you can disable the option, but you have to be sure to remember how — and where — the pattern goes.

 ✔ To remove the pattern lock, set either None or Slide as the type of lock, as described in the earlier section "Finding the lock screens."

 ✔ Wash your hands! Smudge marks on the display can betray your pattern.

Delaying the screen lock

The lock screen shows up right away whenever you unlock your Nexus 7. It also shows up after a *sleep time-out,* or period of inactivity. When that happens, the touchscreen automatically turns off and the tablet locks. You can control the time-out delay for the screen lock as well as whether the tablet locks automatically when you press the Power Lock button.

To see the screen lock time-out delay, get to the Screen Security window: Open the Settings app and choose the Security category. Choose the option Automatically Lock to set how long the touchscreen waits to lock after the Nexus 7 has a sleep time-out. The tablet comes preconfigured with a 5-second delay: If you press the Power Lock button within 5 seconds after a sleep time-out, the lock screen doesn't appear. The value can be adjusted from 0 to 30 minutes.

The Nexus 7 is configured to immediately lock the screen whenever the Power Lock button is pressed. To change this option, remove the check mark by the item Power Button Instantly Locks, also found in the Screen Security window. With this option off, the tablet uses the sleep time-out value to specify when the lock screen kicks in.

Setting a PIN

I suppose that using a PIN, or personal identification number, is more left-brained than using a pattern lock. What's yet another number to memorize?

A *PIN lock* is a code between 4 and 16 numerals long that can contain only the numbers 0 through 9. To set a PIN lock on your Nexus 7, follow the directions in the earlier section "Finding the lock screens" to reach the Choose Screen Lock window. Choose PIN from the list of locks.

Use the onscreen keypad to type your PIN once, and then touch the Continue button. Type the PIN again to confirm that you know it. Touch OK.

The next time you turn on or unlock the Nexus 7, you need to type that PIN to get access.

To disable the PIN, reset the Nexus 7 security level as described in the section "Removing the screen lock," earlier in this chapter.

Assigning a password

The most secure way to lock the Nexus 7 is to apply a full-on pass-word. Unlike a PIN (refer to the preceding section), a *password* can contain numbers, symbols, and either (or both) upper- and lower-case letters.

Set a password by choosing Password from the Choose Screen Lock window; refer to the earlier section "Finding the lock screens" for information on getting to that screen. The password you select must be at least four characters long. Longer passwords are more secure.

You're prompted to type the password whenever you unlock the Nexus 7 or whenever you try to change the screen lock. Touch the OK button to accept the password you've typed.

See the earlier section "Removing the screen lock" for information on resetting the password lock.

Setting the owner info text

You can customize the lock screen by adding some custom text that may help identify your Nexus 7, or simply a pithy saying to entertain yourself. The feature is called Owner Info, so I suppose that the real reason is to type your name and contact info in case your tablet gets lost or stolen.

To set the Owner Info for your Nexus 7, follow these steps:

1. **Visit the Settings app.**
2. **Choose Security.**
3. **Choose Owner Info.**
4. **Ensure that there's a check mark in the box by the option Show Owner Info on Lock Screen.**
5. **Type text into the box.**

    Use the onscreen keyboard to type the text. (Refer to Chapter 3 for typing tips.)

You can type more than one line of text, though only the first five lines of text are fully visible on the lock screen.

6. **Touch the Settings icon in the upper-left corner of the screen when you're done typing.**

Whatever text you type into the box appears on the lock screen. Therefore, I recommend typing something like your name, address, phone number, and e-mail address, for example. This way, should you lose your Nexus 7 and an honest person finds it, they can get it back to you.

The Owner Info shows up when the screen is locked. However, if None is chosen as the screen lock, the information doesn't appear.

Various Adjustments

You have plenty of things to adjust, tune, and tweak on the Nexus 7. The Settings app is the gateway to all those options, and I'm sure that you can waste hours there if you have hours to waste. My guess is that your time is precious; therefore, this section highlights some of the more worthy options and settings.

Singing a different tune

The Sound screen is where you control which sound the Nexus 7 plays for its notification alert, but it's also where you can set the volume and vibration options.

To display the Sound screen, choose Sound from the Settings app screen. You see the Sound screen. Here are some worthy options:

Volumes: Though you can set the Nexus 7 volume by using the Volume buttons on the side of the gizmo, the Volumes command on the Sound screen lets you set the volume for three different types of sound events, as shown in Figure 16-6. Table 16-1 describes the items found in the Volumes window control.

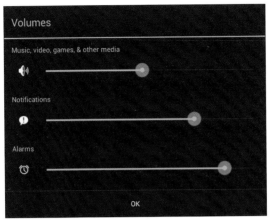

Figure 16-6: Various volume settings.

Table 16-1	Various Noisy Things
Volume Setting	**Sounds That It Controls**
Music, video, and so on	Just about everything that makes noise on the Nexus 7, except for notifications and alarms
Notification	New notifications, such as new e-mail messages, calendar appointments, or whatever else produces an alert
Alarm	Warnings set by the Clock app

For example, if you want the alarms to be loud and all those notification sounds to be rather mute, adjust the sliders (refer to Figure 16-6) accordingly.

Default Notification: Choose which sound you want to hear for a notification alert. Choose a sound, or choose Silent (at the top of the list) for no sound.

 One way to get more sounds into the Nexus 7 is to use an app such as Zedge. When you choose the Default Notification item, you're prompted to choose between Media Storage (the Nexus 7) and Zedge Ringtones. Touch Zedge Ringtones and then the Always button to use Zedge as your source for tablet sounds.

Touch Counts: Put a blue check mark by this item so that you hear a faint click whenever you touch the screen. It's good for feedback.

Screen Lock Sound: I like having this item on because it lets me hear when the screen has locked. Normally, this item isn't selected, so touch the box to put a blue check mark there.

 Another noise item is the Sound On Keypress setting, but you have to choose the Language & Input item in the Settings app to get there. Touch the Settings icon by the Android Keyboard item, and ensure that there's a blue check mark by the item Sound On Keypress.

✔ There's no vibration option on the Nexus 7 — when you silence the tablet, it's truly silent.

✔ You can put the Nexus 7 in Silent mode by pressing the Down Volume button all the way down until the sound is set to zero, or silence.

✔ Unlike on a cell phone, you cannot assign music or your own audio to a Nexus 7 ringtone. Well, unless you use the Zedge app.

Changing visual settings

Probably the key thing you want to adjust visually on the Nexus 7 is screen brightness. In the Settings app, touch the Display entry to view the Display screen. Choose the Brightness item to see the Brightness window.

Move the slider to the left to make the screen dim; move the slider to the right to brighten the screen.

If you place a blue check mark by the Automatic Brightness item, the tablet automatically adjusts its brightness based on the ambient light in the room. Not everyone likes this option, and if that's you, remove the blue check mark by Automatic Brightness and set the brightness manually.

Brightness can also be set by using the Power Control widget, which you can add to the Home screen.

Another item worthy of note is the Sleep setting. Choose this option to see the Sleep menu, from which you can set the inactivity duration, after which the Nexus 7 touchscreen locks itself automatically. I prefer the 10 Minutes value. The tablet is preconfigured for 1 minute.

Chapter 17

Maintenance and Troubleshooting

*M*aintenance for your Nexus 7 is a lot easier than in the old days. Back in the 1970s, tablet computer owners were required to completely disassemble their devices and hand-clean every nut and sprocket with solvent and a wire brush. Special cloth was required to sop up all the electrical oil. It was a nightmare, which is why most people never did maintenance back then.

Today, things are different. Maintenance of your Nexus 7 is rather carefree, involving little more than cleaning the thing every so often. No disassembly is required. Beyond covering maintenance, this chapter offers suggestions for using the battery — plus, it gives you helpful tips and Q&A.

The Maintenance Chore

Relax. Maintenance of the Nexus 7 is simple and quick. Basically, I can summarize it in three words: Keep it clean. Beyond that, another maintenance task worthy of attention is backing up the information stored on your tablet.

Keeping it clean

You probably already keep your Nexus 7 clean. Perhaps you're one of those people who use their sleeves to wipe the touchscreen. Of course, better than your sleeve is something called a *microfiber cloth.* This item can be found at any computer- or office-supply store.

✔ Never use any liquid to clean the touchscreen — especially ammonia or alcohol. These substances damage the touchscreen, rendering it unable to detect your input. Further, such harsh chemicals can smudge the display, making it more difficult to see.

✔ If the screen keeps getting dirty, consider adding a screen protector. This specially designed cover prevents the screen from getting scratched or dirty but also lets you use your finger on the touchscreen. Be sure that the screen protector is designed for use with the Nexus 7.

Backing up your stuff

A *backup* is a safety copy of information. For your Nexus 7, the backup copy includes contact information, music, photos, video, and apps you've installed — plus, any settings you've made to customize your tablet. Copying this information to another source is one way to keep the information safe in case anything happens to your Nexus 7.

Yes, a backup is a good thing. Lamentably, there's no universal method of backing up the stuff on your Nexus 7.

Your Google account information is backed up automatically. That information includes your address book (from the People app), Gmail inbox, and Calendar app appointments. Because the information automatically syncs with the Internet, a backup is always present.

To confirm that your Google account information is being backed up, heed these steps:

1. **At the Home screen, touch the All Apps button.**

2. **Choose Settings.**

3. **Choose Google from beneath the Accounts heading.**

4. **Touch the green Sync button by your Google account name.**

5. **Ensure that blue check marks appear by every item in the list.**

   Yeah, there are a lot of items. They all need blue check marks if you want those items backed up.

6. **Touch the Back navigation button twice to return to the main Settings app screen.**

7. **Choose Backup & Reset.**

8. **Ensure that a check mark appears by the item Back Up My Data.**

   You should see a blue check mark there. If not, touch the square to add one.

Beyond your Google account, which is automatically backed up, the rest of the information can be manually backed up. You can copy files from the tablet's internal storage to your computer as a form of backup. See Chapter 14 for information on manually copying files and folders between the Nexus 7 and your computer.

Yes, I agree: Manual backup isn't an example of technology making your life easier.

 A backup of the data stored on the Nexus 7 would include all data, including photos, videos, and music. Specifically, the folders you should copy are DCIM, Download, and Music. Additional folders to copy include folders named after apps you've downloaded, such as Aldiko, Kindle, Kobo, layar, and other folders named after the apps that created them.

Updating the system

Every so often, a new version of the Nexus 7's operating system becomes available. It's an *Android* update because Android is the name of the operating system, not because the Nexus 7 thinks that it's a type of robot.

When an automatic update occurs, you see an alert or a message appear, indicating that a system upgrade is available. You usually have three options:

✔ Install Now

✔ Install Later

✔ More Info

My advice is to choose Install Now and get it over with — unless you're doing something urgent, in which case you can put off the update until later by choosing Install Later.

✔ If possible, connect the Nexus 7 to a power source during an update.

✔ Some updates may present only one option: Restart & Install. Choose it.

✔ You can manually check for updates: In the Settings app, choose About Tablet and then choose System Updates. When your system is up-to-date, the screen tells you so. Otherwise, you find directions for updating the Android operating system.

✔ Touching the Check Now button isn't magic. If an update is available, the tablet lets you know.

✔ Non-Android system updates might also be issued. For example, Asus (the tablet's manufacturer) may send out an update to the Nexus 7's guts. This type of update is often called a *firmware* update. As with Android updates, my advice is to accept all firmware updates.

Battery Care and Feeding

Perhaps the most important item you can monitor and maintain on your Nexus 7 is its battery. The battery supplies the necessary electrical juice by which the device operates. Without battery power, your tablet is basically an expensive trivet. Keep an eye on the battery.

Monitoring the battery

You can find information about the Nexus 7's battery status in the upper-right corner of the screen, in the status area, next to the time. The icons used to display battery status are shown in Figure 17-1.

You might also see an icon for a dead battery, but for some reason I can't get my Nexus 7 to turn on and display the icon.

The next section describes features that consume battery power and how to deal with battery issues. It also shows a more accurate way to gauge how much battery power is left.

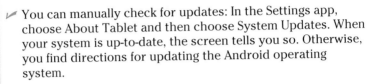

Heed those low-battery warnings! The Nexus 7 alerts you whenever the battery level gets low, at about 15 percent capacity. You see a warning on the screen, urging you to connect to a power supply at once.

Battery is fully charged, and the Nexus 7 is happy.

Battery is starting to drain.

Battery is low. You're urged to charge soon.

Battery is very low. Stop using and charge at once!

Battery is being charged.

Figure 17-1: Battery status icons.

Another warning appears when the battery level sinks below 5 percent, but why wait for that? Take action at the 15 percent warning.

- The battery status is also found on the Quick Actions shade.
- When the battery level is too low, the Nexus 7 shuts itself off.

- The best way to deal with low battery power is to connect the tablet to a power source: Either plug it into a wall socket, or connect it to a computer by using a USB cable. The Nexus 7 begins charging itself immediately; plus, you can use the device while it's charging.

- You don't have to fully charge the Nexus 7 to use it. When you have only 20 minutes to charge and you get only a 70 percent battery level, that's great. Well, it's not great, but it's far better than a lower battery level.

- Battery percentage values are best-guess estimates. The Nexus 7 has a hearty battery that can last for hours. But when the battery meter gets low, the battery drains faster. So, if you get 8 hours of use from the tablet and the battery meter shows 20 percent left, those numbers don't imply that 20 percent equals 2 more hours of use. In practice, the amount of time you have left is much less. As a rule, when the battery percentage value gets low, the battery appears to drain faster.

Determining what is sucking up power

The Nexus 7 is smart enough to know which of its features and apps use the most battery power. You can check it out for yourself:

1. **At the Home screen, touch the All Apps button.**

2. **Choose Settings.**

3. **Choose Battery.**

   You see a screen similar to the one shown in Figure 17-2.

Usage and time chart

Current battery charge and state

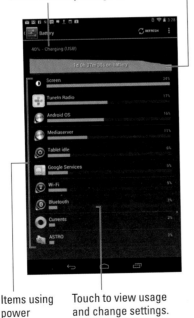

Items using power

Touch to view usage and change settings.

Figure 17-2: Things that drain the battery.

The number and variety of items listed on the Battery screen depend on what you've been doing between charges and how many apps you're using.

Carefully note which applications consume the most battery power. You can curb your use of these programs to conserve juice — though, honestly, your savings are negligible. See the next section for battery-saving advice.

~ You can touch any item listed on the Battery screen to see further details for that item. On the Use Details screen, you can review what specifically is drawing power. Buttons are available on some screens that let you disable features that may be drawing too much power.

~ Not everything you've done shows up on the Battery Use screen. (Refer to Figure 17-2.) For example, even after I read a Kindle book for about half an hour, Kindle didn't show up. Also, I've seen the Gallery app show up from time to time, even though I've not used it.

Extending battery life

A surefire way to make a battery last a good, long time is to never turn on the device in the first place. That's kind of impractical, so rather than let you use your Nexus 7 as an expensive paperweight, I offer a smattering of suggestions you can follow to help prolong battery life in your Nexus 7:

Lower the volume: Additionally, consider lowering the volume for the various noises the Nexus 7 makes, especially notifications. Information on setting volume options is also found in Chapter 16.

Dim the screen: If you look at Figure 17-2 (earlier in this chapter), you see that the display (labeled Screen) sucks down quite a lot of battery power. Though a dim screen can be more difficult to see, especially outdoors, it definitely saves on battery life.

Turn off Bluetooth: When you're not using Bluetooth, turn it off. See Chapter 13 for information on Bluetooth.

Turn off Wi-Fi: Because I tend to use Wi-Fi in only one spot, I keep the tablet plugged in. Away from a single location, however, Wi-Fi "wanders" and isn't useful for an Internet connection anyway. So why not turn it off? Refer to Chapter 13 for information on Wi-Fi.

Disable GPS: The GPS services are handy for finding yourself and places nearby, but they too use a lot of power. Disable the GPS by choosing the Location Services item in the Settings app. Remove all the blue check marks. Also see Chapter 9 for information on the location services.

Help and Troubleshooting

Wouldn't it be great if you could have an avuncular Mr. Wizard-type available at a moment's notice? He could just walk in and, with a happy smile on his face and a reassuring hand on your shoulder, let you know what the problem is and how to fix it. Then he'd give you a cookie. Never mind that such a thing would be creepy — getting helpful advice is worth it.

Fixing random and annoying problems

Here are some typical problems you may encounter on the Nexus 7 and my suggestions for a solution:

General trouble: For just about any problem or minor quirk, consider restarting the Nexus 7: Turn it off, and then turn it on again. This procedure will most likely fix a majority of the annoying problems you encounter.

Check the Wi-Fi connection: Ensure that the Wi-Fi network is set up properly and working. This process usually involves pestering the person who configured the Wi-Fi router or, in a coffee shop, bothering the cheerful person with the bad haircut who serves you coffee.

Reset the Wi-Fi connection: Perhaps the issue isn't with the Nexus 7, but rather with the Wi-Fi network. Some networks have a "lease time" after which your tablet might be disconnected. If so, follow the directions in Chapter 13 for turning off the tablet's Wi-Fi and then turn it on again. This technique often solves the issue.

Music is playing, and you want it to stop: It's awesome that the Nexus 7 continues to play music while you do other things. Getting the music to stop quickly, however, requires some skill. You can access the play controls for the Play Music app from a number of locations. They're found on the lock screen, for example. You can also find them by pulling down the notifications shade.

An app has run amok: Sometimes, apps that misbehave let you know. You see a Sorry warning on the screen announcing the app's stubborn disposition. When that happens, touch the Force Close button to shut down the errant app.

When you see no warning or an app appears to be unduly obstinate, you can shut 'er down the manual way, by following these steps:

1. **Open the Settings app.**

2. **Choose Apps.**

3. **Select the Running category from the top of the screen.**

   You can swipe the screen to the left to get to the category from the Downloaded category.

4. **Choose the app that's causing you distress.**

   For example, a program doesn't start or says that it's busy or has another issue.

5. **Touch the Stop button.**

   The app stops.

6. **After stopping the app, try opening it again to see whether it works.**

   If the app continues to run amok, contact its developer: Continue with Step 7. Otherwise, you've fixed the problem.

7. **Open the Play Store app.**

8. **Touch the My Apps button at the top of the screen.**

9. **Choose the app you're having trouble with.**

10. **Scroll down to the Developer section, and choose the Send Email item.**

11. **Send the developer a message describing the problem.**

 Reset the Nexus 7 software: When all else fails, you can do the drastic thing and reset all tablet software, essentially returning it to the state it was in when it first popped out of the box. Obviously, you need not perform this step lightly. In fact, consider finding support (see the later section "Getting support") before you start the following process:

1. **Start the Settings app.**

2. **Choose Backup & Reset.**

3. **Choose Factory Data Reset.**

4. **Touch the Reset Tablet button.**

5. Touch the Erase Everything button to confirm.

All the information you've set or stored on the Nexus 7 is purged. It includes apps you've downloaded, music, synchronized accounts, everything.

Again, do not follow these steps unless you're certain that they will fix the problem or you're under orders to do so from someone in Tech Support.

 You can also choose to reset the Nexus 7's software and erase everything if you ever return or sell your Nexus 7. Of course, you probably love your Nexus 7 so much that the mere thought of selling it makes you blanch.

Using the "manual"

Don't bother looking inside the box again. It has no printed manual for the Nexus 7. True, a *Quick Start Guide* is in the box, but the documentation (which is what the manual is called these days) is provided for you as a Google Play book, included on the tablet. It's the *Nexus 7 Guidebook.* published by Google, and it was probably written by the Android robot himself.

To read the manual, open the Play Books app. Choose the *Nexus 7 Guidebook.* Remark to yourself how dry and humorless it is.

See Chapter 11 for information on reading eBooks on the Nexus 7.

Getting support

Before you contact someone about support, it helps to know the device's ID and Android operating system version number:

1. At the Home screen, touch the All Apps button.

2. Choose Settings.

3. Choose About Tablet.

The Nexus 7 model number is listed, as well as its Android version.

Jot down the model number and Android version! Do it right here:

Model Number: _____

Android Version: _____

Online support is provided by Google:

```
support.google.com/googleplay/devices
```

You can send e-mail questions or simply read some questions and answers online. If you need to phone tech support, dial (855) 836-3987.

Valuable Nexus 7 Q&A

I love Q&A! That's because not only is it an effective way to express certain problems and solutions, but some of the questions might also cover things I've been wanting to ask.

"I can't turn the tablet on (or off)!"

Yes, sometimes the Nexus 7 locks up. It's frustrating, but I've discovered that if you press and hold the Power button for about 8 seconds, the tablet turns either off or on, depending on which state it's in.

I've had a program lock the Nexus 7 tight when the 8-second power switch trick didn't work. In that case, I waited 12 minutes or so, just letting the tablet sit there and do nothing. Then I pressed and held the Power button for about 8 seconds, and it turned itself back on.

"The touchscreen doesn't work!"

A touchscreen, such as the one used on the Nexus 7, requires a human finger for proper interaction. The tablet interprets the static potential between the human finger and the device to determine where the touchscreen is being touched.

You cannot use the touchscreen when you're wearing gloves, unless they're specially designed, static-carrying gloves that claim to work on touchscreens.

The touchscreen might also fail when the battery power is low or when the Nexus 7 has been physically damaged.

I've been informed that there's an Android app for cats. This implies that the touchscreen can also interpret a feline paw for proper interaction. Either that, or the cat can hold a human finger in its mouth and manipulate the app that way. Because I don't have the app, I can't tell for certain.

"The battery doesn't charge!"

Start from the source: Is the wall socket providing power? Is the cord plugged in? The cable may be damaged, so try another cable.

When charging from a USB port on a computer, ensure that the computer is turned on. Most computers don't provide USB power when they're turned off.

"The tablet gets so hot that it turns itself off!"

Yikes! An overheating gadget can be a nasty problem. Judge how hot the Nexus 7 is by seeing whether you can hold it in your hand: When it's too hot to hold, it's too hot. If you're using the Nexus 7 to cook an egg, it's too hot.

Turn off the Nexus 7 and let the battery cool.

If the overheating problem continues, have the Nexus 7 looked at for potential repair. The battery might need to be replaced, and as far as I can tell, there's no way to remove and replace the Nexus 7 battery by yourself.

Do not continue to use any gizmo that's too hot! The heat damages the electronics. It can also start a fire.

"The tablet doesn't do Landscape mode!"

Not every app takes advantage of the Nexus 7's ability to orient itself in Landscape mode, or even upside-down mode. For example, many games set their orientations one way and refuse to change, no matter how you hold the tablet. So just because the app doesn't go into Landscape mode doesn't mean that anything is broken.

Confirm that the orientation lock isn't on: Pull down the Quick Actions shade, and ensure that the Auto Rotate item isn't locked; otherwise, the screen doesn't reorient itself.

Part V
The Part of Tens

The 5th Wave   By Rich Tennant

"Okay, antidote, antidote, what would an antidote app look like?"

In this part . . .

Welcome to the last part of the book, assuming that you've read this book sequentially, which I warned you in the introduction not to do. This is the traditional last part of a *For Dummies* book, the part that lists chapters containing ten items each. The contents vary. *Home Surgery For Dummies* has a chapter titled "Ten Quick Surgeries Using a Can Opener and Tweezers"; *Pencils For Dummies* has "Ten Ways to Sharpen a Pencil When You're Lost in Nature"; and *Pirates For Dummies* offers "Ten Things Pirates Say Besides 'Argh!'"

In this book as well, you'll find the traditional Part of Tens. Here, you'll find chapters that range from the interesting to the necessary to the highly useful, each chapter containing exactly ten items.

Chapter 18

Ten Tips, Tricks, and Shortcuts

A tip is a small suggestion, a word of advice often spoken from experience or knowledge. A *trick,* which is something not many know, usually causes amazement or surprise. A *shortcut* is a quick way to get home, even though it crosses the old graveyard and you never quite know whether Old Man Witherspoon is the groundskeeper or a zombie.

I'd like to think that just about everything in this book is a tip, trick, or shortcut for using the Nexus 7. Even so, I've distilled a list of items in this chapter that are definitely worthy of note.

Widgets on the Lock Screen

Just as you can adorn the Home screen with widgets, you can also slap down a few right on the Lock screen. In fact, the time display on the Nexus 7's Lock screen is really a widget. It's only one of several.

To add a Lock screen widget, touch the large plus button that appears on the Lock screen. If you don't see that button, swipe the screen left or right. Choose a widget to add from the list displayed, such as the Calendar, Gmail, Digital Clock, or other widgets.

✔ Multiple widgets can be placed on the Lock screen, though you can see only one at a time. Swipe the screen to see others.

✔ To remove a Lock screen widget, long-press it. Drag the widget up to the Remove icon and it's gone. You can even remove the Clock widget, in which case only the large plus button appears on the Lock screen.

Summon a Recently Opened App

I have to kick myself in the head every time I return to the All Apps screen to, once again, page through the panels o' icons to dig up an app I just opened. Why bother? Because I can summon the list of recently opened apps by touching the Recent Apps navigation button at the bottom of the Home screen.

Using the Recent Apps button is the best way you can switch between two running apps. When you need to switch, for example, between Email and Chrome, just touch the Recent Apps button and choose the bottom item on the list. It's effectively the same thing as the Alt+Tab key combination in Windows.

Friendly Friend Buttons

You'll find your friends handy, seeing them appear in many of the apps on your Nexus 7. When you see one — well, either their smiling face in a picture or the generic-person icon — you may find a teensy menu button in the lower-right corner. Touching the button (shown in the margin) displays a pop-up window with some contract detail, as shown in Figure 18-1.

Contact quick tasks

Quick-task details   Show contact
(in People app).

Figure 18-1: More info for a contact.

In addition to the contact's name, you see a row of quick-task icons just below the picture. Each of the icons represents an action you can take to deal with the contact. The number and variety of actions depend on the details provided for the contact in the People app.

In Figure 18-1, icons are shown (from left to right) for Email, Google+, Google Talk, Maps, and Chrome. The Email icon is selected in Figure 18-1, so the contact's various e-mail addresses (only one in the figure) are displayed. Choose an address to start either the Gmail or Email app, and compose a message. Or touch the Map icon to choose a location, such as work or home, to go visit that person and ask for the money they owe you.

The more details you supply in the People app for your friends, the more you can do with those friends on your Nexus 7.

Add a Contact Screen Widget

The people you contact most often are deserving of their own contact shortcuts on the Home screen. You just don't realize how useful such a thing is until you have one.

To create a contact screen shortcut, follow these steps:

1. **Touch the All Apps button on the Home screen.**

2. **Choose the Widgets category from the top of the screen.**

3. **Scroll the Widget category until you find the contact widgets.**

   The two contact widgets are different in size. One is three icon widths wide; the other is one. Both are one icon width tall.

4. **Long-press a contact widget, and drag it to the Home screen.**

5. **Choose a contact from the tablet's address book, someone to assign to that widget.**

   The widget represents the contact, giving you handy access to their information from the Home screen.

When you touch the contact widget, you see a pop-up window, similar to the one shown in Figure 18-1. Choose an activity for that contact, such as sending an e-mail.

Watch the Tablet Dream

Does the Nexus 7 fall asleep or does it just lock? A locked tablet seems rather restrictive, so I prefer to think of the tablet as taking a snooze. But does it dream? Of course it does! You can even see the dreams, providing you activate the Daydream feature — and you keep the tablet connected to a power source or in a docking station. Heed these steps:

1. **Start the Settings app.**

2. **Choose Display–>Daydream.**

3. **Ensure that the Daydream switch is in the On position.**

4. **Choose which type of daydream you want displayed.**

   The Clock is a popular item, though I'm fond of Colors.

   Some daydream items feature a Settings button, which can be used to customize how the daydream appears.

5. **Touch the When to Daydream button.**

6. **Choose the Either option**

7. **Touch the Back or Home buttons when you're done configuring the Daydream feature.**

The daydreaming begins when the screen would normally timeout and lock. So if you've set the tablet to lock after 5 minutes of inactivity, it daydreams instead.

✔ To disrupt the tablet's dreaming, swipe the screen.

✔ The Nexus 7 doesn't lock when it daydreams. To lock the tablet, press the Power Lock button.

Add Another User

Computers have had the ability to allow multiple users for some time — even though I don't believe anyone really uses that feature. The whole motif of the personal computer is supposed to be one computer, one person, right? Your Nexus 7 should be the same, but just like your computer you can have more than one user account on your tablet.

Over my objections, the Nexus 7 allows you to configure multiple users — several people who can have their own, custom Home screen, widgets, and other options on a single tablet.

To add another user for the Nexus 7, open the Settings app and choose Users. Touch the Add User button, touch OK, then touch the Set Up Now button to configure the user. Or hand the tablet to the other user and let them configure it. The configuration process is basically the same setup procedure you suffered through when you first turned on the Nexus 7.

All accounts added to your Nexus 7 appear at the bottom of the Lock screen. To have someone else use the tablet, lock the screen and then have the other user unlock the tablet. Touch the user account circle at the bottom of the screen to use the tablet as that person.

✔ I highly recommend that you apply a PIN or password to your account if you're going to have multiple users on the Nexus 7.

✔ The Nexus 7's first user (most likely you) is the main user, the one who has primary administrative control.

✔ When you're done using the tablet, lock the screen. Other users can then access their own accounts

✔ You can check to see which account you're using on the Nexus 7 by pulling down the Quick Actions shade. The current user is shown in the shade's upper-left corner.

☞ Remove an account by visiting the Users screen in the Settings app. Touch the Trash icon next to an account to remove it. Touch the Delete button to confirm.

☞ I don't like having separate users on my Nexus 7. It makes a simple device complicated. With the tablet's low cost, it just makes more sense to have a second user get his own Nexus 7.

Add Spice to Dictation

I feel that too few people use dictation, despite how handy it can be. Whether or not you use it, you might notice that it occasionally censors some of the words you utter. Perhaps you're the kind of person who doesn't put up with that kind of s***.

Relax, b******. You can lift the vocal censorship ban by following these steps:

1. **Open the Settings app.**

2. **Choose Language & Input.**

3. **Touch the Settings icon by the item Google Voice Typing.**

4. **Remove the check mark by the option Block Offensive Words.**

And just what are offensive words? I would think that *censorship* would be an offensive word. But no, apparently the words s***, c***, and even innocent little old a****** are deemed offensive by Google Voice. What the h***?

Enter Location Information for Your Events

When you create an event for the Calendar app, be sure to enter the event location. You can type either an address (if you know it) or the name of the location. The key is to type the text as you would type it in the Maps app when searching for a location. That way, you can touch the event location, and the Nexus 7 displays it on the touchscreen. Finding an appointment couldn't be easier.

☞ See Chapter 9 for more information about the Maps app.

☞ See Chapter 11 for details about the Calendar.

Use the Task Manager

Some Android phones and tablets come with a Task Manager, which you can use to examine the list of running apps and halt apps run amok. The Nexus 7 has no specific task manager app, but it does have a list of running apps that does almost the same thing.

To view running apps on your tablet, follow these steps:

1. **Open the Settings app.**

2. **Choose the Apps item.**

3. **Choose the Running category.**

   You see a list of apps currently active on your Nexus 7, similar to what's shown in Figure 18-2. Some of the items are apps, such as Google Play Magazines, shown in the figure, but others are services, such as the Media service. Some apps may even have double entries, showing that the apps are doing more than one thing at a time.

Running apps

Memory usage   Details

Figure 18-2: Apps running on the Nexus 7.

4. **Choose an app to examine more details.**

The details break down the app's usage of the tablet's resources into an organized list of exhaustive information that few people understand.

When examining an item, you can touch the Stop button to halt that app or service. Even though this process is necessary to halt apps run amok, I don't recommend that you go about and randomly stop apps and services. The end result could render the tablet unstable, requiring you to power off or reset to regain control.

Find Your Lost Nexus 7

Someday, you may lose your Nexus 7. It might be for a panic-filled few seconds, or it might be for forever. The hardware solution is to weld a heavy object to the tablet, such as a bowling ball or furnace, yet that kind of defeats the entire mobile/wireless paradigm. The software solution is to use a cell phone locator service.

Even though the Nexus 7 isn't a cell phone, you can use the same apps that cell phones use to help find a wayward Nexus 7. Those apps use the cellular signal as well as the tablet's GPS to help locate a missing gizmo.

Many apps available at the Google Play Store can help locate your Nexus 7. I've not tried them all. Here are some suggestions:

- Plan B from Lookout Mobile Security
- Norton Mobile Security
- Security Pro

Most of these services require that you set up a web page account to assist in locating your Nexus 7. They also enable services that send updates to the Internet. The updates assist in tracking your Nexus 7, in case it becomes lost or is stolen.

Chapter 19

Ten Things to Remember

In This Chapter

- Speaking to the Nexus 7
- Turning the tablet sideways
- Locking orientation
- Improving your typing with suggestions
- Minding the battery hogs
- Getting a docking station
- Making phone calls
- Checking your schedule
- Taking a picture of a contact
- Using the Search command

*H*ave you ever tried to tie string around your finger to remember something? I've not attempted that technique just yet. The main reason is that I keep forgetting to buy string and I have no way to remind myself.

For your Nexus 7, some things are definitely worth remembering. Out of the long, long list, I've come up with ten good ones.

Use Dictation

It's such a handy feature, yet I constantly forget to use it: Rather than type text, use dictation. You can access dictation from any onscreen keyboard by touching the Microphone button. Speak the text; the text appears. Simple.

The key to dictation is to look for the Microphone button, shown in the margin, on the onscreen keyboard. Touch the button and talk. See Chapter 3 for more information on Nexus 7 dictation.

Landscape Orientation

Apps such as Chrome, Play Books, and even Email can look much better in the horizontal orientation. Likewise, it's easier to read a conversation in the chatting apps, such as Google Talk, when things are narrow. Simply turn the tablet over on its side and start reading.

✔ Not every app supports portrait orientation. Some apps — specifically, some games — appear only in landscape orientation.

✔ Some apps, such as Play Books, have screen rotation settings that let you lock the orientation to the way you want regardless of what the tablet is doing.

Orientation Lock

The opposite of remembering that the Nexus 7 has landscape orientation (see the preceding section) is forgetting that it has the orientation lock feature. When engaged, the orientation lock prevents the screen from adjusting between Landscape and Portrait modes: The screen stays fixed in whichever orientation it was in when you set the orientation lock.

To set the orientation lock, pull down the Quick Actions shade and ensure that the Auto Rotate icon is locked; the button says Rotation Locked when it's active. See Chapter 2 for details.

Use the Keyboard Suggestions

Don't forget to take advantage of the suggestions that appear above the onscreen keyboard when you're typing text. In fact, you don't even need to touch a suggestion: To replace your text with the highlighted suggestion, simply touch the onscreen keyboard's Space key. Zap! The word appears.

To ensure that suggestions are enabled, follow these steps:

1. **Start the Settings app.**

2. **Choose Language & Input.**

3. **Touch the Settings icon by the Android Keyboard item.**

4. **Ensure that a check mark appears by the Next-Word Suggestions item.**

Also refer to Chapter 3 for additional information on using the keyboard suggestions.

Things That Consume Lots of Battery Juice

Four items on the Nexus 7 suck down battery power faster than a massive alien fleet is defeated by a plucky antihero who just wants the girl:

- Wi-Fi networking
- Bluetooth
- GPS
- Navigation

Wi-Fi networking, Bluetooth, and GPS all require extra power for their wireless radios. The amount isn't much, but it's enough that I would consider shutting them down when battery power gets low.

Navigation is certainly handy, but because the Nexus 7 touchscreen is on the entire time and dictating text to you, the battery drains rapidly. If possible, try to plug the tablet into the car's power socket when you're navigating.

See Chapter 17 for more information on managing the Nexus 7's battery.

Use a Docking Stand

As this book goes to press, the official Nexus 7 docking stand isn't available. It will be worth the wait. A docking stand is a helpful way to hold the tablet, to keep it propped up and easy to use. The stand makes a great home base for the tablet — you'll always know where it is, even on the messiest desk with the most storm-tossed sea of paper.

Depending on what's available in the future, the docking stand may also provide access for USB mice and keyboards, and even an HDMI output for connecting the tablet to a large-screen TV or monitor.

Make Phone Calls

Yeah, I know: It's not a phone. The Nexus 7 lacks the native ability to use the cellular data system for Internet access, let alone make phone calls. Why let that stop you?

Using apps such as Talk and Skype, you can place phone calls and video-chat with your friends. Skype even lets you dial into "real" phones, if you boost your account with some Skype Credit. See Chapter 8 for details.

Mind Your Schedule

The Calendar app can certainly be handy to remind you of upcoming dates and generally keep you on schedule. A useful way to augment the calendar is to employ the Calendar widget on the Home screen.

The Calendar widget lists the current date and then a long list of upcoming appointments. It's a simple way to check your schedule, especially when you use your tablet all the time. I recommend sticking the Calendar widget right on the center Home screen panel.

See Chapter 16 for information on adding widgets to the Home screen; Chapter 11 covers the Calendar app.

Snap a Pic of That Contact

Here's something I always forget: Whenever you're near one of your contacts, take the person's picture. Sure, some people are bashful, but most folks are flattered. The idea is to build up your tablet's address book so that all contacts have photos.

Because the Nexus 7 has only a front-facing camera, simply access the person's entry in the People app. Edit the entry and access the photo. Then you can hand the tablet to your contact and have them take their own picture. This process avoids any potential anger resulting from your snapping their picture without their knowing.

See Chapter 4 for more information on using the People app.

The Search Command

Google is known worldwide for its searching abilities. By gum, the word *Google* is now synonymous with searching. So please don't forget that the Nexus 7, which uses the Google Android operating system, has a powerful Search command.

The Search command is not only powerful but also available all over. You can touch the Search icon button in any app where you can find it. Use it to search for information, locations, people — you name it. It's handy.

Don't forget about Google Now, which makes voice searching a snap. See Chapter 11.

Chapter 20

Ten Great Apps

*M*ore than 500,000 apps are available at the Google Play Store — so many that it would take you more than a relaxing evening to discover them all. Rather than list every single app, I've culled from the lot some apps that I find exceptional — that show the diversity of the Google Play Store but also how well the Nexus 7 can run Android apps.

Every app listed in this chapter is free; see Chapter 12 for directions on finding them using the Google Play Store.

AK Notepad

One program that the Nexus 7 is missing out of the box is a notepad. A good choice for an app to fill the void is AK Notepad: You can type or dictate short messages and memos, which I find handy.

For example, before a recent visit to the hardware store, I made (dictated) a list of items I needed by using AK Notepad. I also keep important items as notes — things that I often forget or don't care to remember, such as frequent flyer numbers, cartridges for my laser printer, dress shirt and suit size (like I ever need that info), and other important info that I might need handy but not cluttering my brain.

ASTRO File Manager

Another program the Nexus 7 is missing is a file manager. True, not everyone is a total nerd and wants a file manager. So I'm not talking to you if you're a non-nerd. But for many things you do on the tablet, it's handy to be able to peel back the operating system's veneer and get into its ugly, file-folder guts. ASTRO is the perfect tool.

As a bonus, ASTRO can also be used to access files on your Wi-Fi network. It takes some configuration, which isn't the easiest thing, but once it's set up, you can use the app to access your computer over your Wi-Fi network.

Dropbox

One solid way to share files between your computer, laptop, and tablet is to use the file sharing and synchronizing utility Dropbox. You need to obtain an account at the `https://www.dropbox.com` website. Then the Dropbox software must be installed on your computer to share files there. When that's done, you can get the Dropbox app for your Nexus 7 to access and view those shared files.

With Dropbox, there's no need to synchronize files between your computer and your tablet. Any files stored in the Dropbox folders are automatically synchronized.

Google Finance

The Google Finance app is an excellent market-tracking tool for folks who are obsessed with the stock market or who want to keep an eye on their portfolios. The app offers an overview of the market and updates to your stocks as well as links to financial news.

To get the most from this app, configure Google Finance on the web, using your computer. You can create lists of stocks to watch, which are then instantly synchronized with your Nexus 7. You can visit Google Finance on the web at

```
www.google.com/finance
```

As with other Google services, Google Finance is provided to you for free, as part of your Google account.

Google Sky Map

Ever look up into the night sky and ask, "What the heck is that?" Unless it's a bird, an airplane, a satellite, or a UFO, the Google Sky Map can help you find what it is. You may discover that a particularly bright star in the sky is, in fact, the planet Jupiter.

The Google Sky Map app is elegant. It basically turns the Nexus 7 into a window you can look through to identify things in the night sky. Just start the app and hold the Nexus 7 up to the sky. Pan the tablet to identify planets, stars, and constellations.

 Google Sky Map promotes using the Nexus 7 without touching it. For this reason, the screen goes blank after a spell, which is merely the tablet's power-saving mode. If you plan extensive stargazing with Google Sky Map, consider resetting the sleep time-out. Refer to Chapter 16 for information on this topic.

Movies

The Movies app is the Nexus 7's gateway to Hollywood. It lists currently running films and films that are opening, and it has links to your local theaters with showtimes and other information. The app is also tied into the popular Rotten Tomatoes website for reviews and feedback. If you enjoy going to the movies, you'll find the Movies app a valuable addition to your Nexus 7's app library.

SportsTap

I admit to not being a sports nut, so it's difficult for me to identify with the craving to have the latest scores, news, and schedules. The sports nuts in my life, however, tell me that the very best app for that purpose is a handy thing named SportsTap.

Rather than blather on about something I'm not into, just take my advice and obtain SportsTap. I believe you'll be thrilled.

TuneIn Radio

I realize that I mention this app over in Chapter 10, but I really do recommend it. One of my favorite ways that the Nexus 7 entertains me is as a little radio I keep by my workstation. I use the TuneIn Radio app to find a favorite Internet radio station, and then I sit back and work.

While TuneIn Radio is playing, you can do other things with your tablet, such as check Facebook or answer an e-mail. You can return to the TuneIn Radio app by choosing its notification icon. Or just keep it going and enjoy the tunes.

Voice Recorder

The Nexus 7 can record your voice or other sounds, and the Voice Recorder is a good app for performing this task. It has an elegant and simple interface: Touch the big Record button to start recording. Make a note for yourself or record a friend doing his Daffy Duck impression.

WARNING

Avoiding Android viruses

How can you tell which apps are legitimate and which might be viruses or evil apps that do odd things to your tablet? Well, you can't. In fact, most people can't, because most evil apps don't advertise themselves as such.

The key to knowing whether an app is evil is to look at what it does, as described in Chapter 12. If a simple grocery list app uses the phone's text messaging service and the app doesn't need to send text messages, for example, it's suspect.

In the history of the Android operating system, only a handful of malicious apps have been distributed, and most of them were discovered in Asia. Google routinely removes these apps from the Google Play Store, and a feature of the Android operating system even lets Google remove apps from your tablet. So you're pretty safe.

Generally speaking, avoid "hacker" apps, porn, and apps that use social engineering to make you do things on your Nexus 7 that you wouldn't otherwise do. Avoid the temptation to get an app just because it offers something salacious or titillating.

Also, I highly recommend that you abstain from obtaining apps from anything but the official Google Play Store. The Amazon Market is okay, but some other markets are basically distribution points for illegal or infected software. Avoid them.

Previous recordings are stored in a list on the Voice Recorder's main screen. Each recording is shown with its title, the date and time of the recording, and the recording duration.

Many Voice Recorder apps are out there. The one I'm recommending is from Mamoru Tokashiki.

Zedge

The Zedge program is a helpful resource for finding wallpapers and ringtones — millions of them. It's a sharing app, so you can access wallpapers and ringtones created by other Android users as well as share your own. If you're looking for a specific sound or something special for Home screen wallpaper, Zedge is the best place to start your search.

Index

• *N* •

Contra Costa County Library
El Sobrante
5/9/2017 2:58:59 PM

- Patron Receipt -
- Charges -

ID: 21901021324896

Item: 31901049422035
Title: Last train home
Call Number: DVD 331.54409 LAST
Due Date: 5/30/2017

Item: 31901036913046
Title: The crochet answer book /
Call Number: 746.434 ECKMAN
Due Date: 5/30/2017

Item: 31901051970301
Title: Nexus 7 for dummies /
Call Number: 004.165 GOOKIN 2013
Due Date: 5/30/2017

All Contra Costa County Libraries will be
closed on April 16th, May 14th, May 28th,
and May 29th. Items may be renewed online
at ccclib.org or by calling 1-800-984-4636,
menu option 1. Book drops will be open.
----- **Please keep this slip** -----

Apple & Macs

iPad For Dummies
978-0-470-58027-1

iPhone For Dummies,
4th Edition
978-0-470-87870-5

MacBook For
Dummies, 3rd Edition
978-0-470-76918-8

Mac OS X Snow
Leopard For
Dummies
978-0-470-43543-4

Business

Bookkeeping For
Dummies
978-0-7645-9848-7

Job Interviews
For Dummies,
3rd Edition
978-0-470-17748-8

Resumes For
Dummies,
5th Edition
978-0-470-08037-5

Starting an
Online Business
For Dummies,
6th Edition
978-0-470-60210-2

Stock Investing
For Dummies,
3rd Edition
978-0-470-40114-9

Successful
Time Management
For Dummies
978-0-470-29034-7

Computer Hardware

BlackBerry
For Dummies,
4th Edition
978-0-470-60700-8

Computers For
Seniors
For Dummies,
2nd Edition
978-0-470-53483-0

PCs For Dummies,
Windows 7 Edition
978-0-470-46542-4

Laptops For
Dummies,
4th Edition
978-0-470-57829-2

Cooking & Entertaining

Cooking Basics
For Dummies,
3rd Edition
978-0-7645-7206-7

Wine For Dummies,
4th Edition
978-0-470-04579-4

Diet & Nutrition

Dieting For Dummies,
2nd Edition
978-0-7645-4149-0

Nutrition For
Dummies,
4th Edition
978-0-471-79868-2

Weight Training
For Dummies,
3rd Edition
978-0-471-76845-6

Digital Photography

Digital SLR Cameras
& Photography For
Dummies, 3rd Edition
978-0-470-46606-3

Photoshop Elements 8
For Dummies
978-0-470-52967-6

Gardening

Gardening Basics
For Dummies
978-0-470-03749-2

Organic Gardening
For Dummies,
2nd Edition
978-0-470-43067-5

Green/Sustainable

Raising Chickens
For Dummies
978-0-470-46544-8

Green Cleaning
For Dummies
978-0-470-39106-8

Health

Diabetes For
Dummies,
3rd Edition
978-0-470-27086-8

Food Allergies
For Dummies
978-0-470-09584-3

Living Gluten-Free
For Dummies,
2nd Edition
978-0-470-58589-4

Hobbies/General

Chess For Dummies,
2nd Edition
978-0-7645-8404-6

Drawing
Cartoons & Comics
For Dummies
978-0-470-42683-8

Knitting For Dummies,
2nd Edition
978-0-470-28747-7

Organizing
For Dummies
978-0-7645-5300-4

Su Doku For
Dummies
978-0-470-01892-7

Home Improvement

Home Maintenance
For Dummies,
2nd Edition
978-0-470-43063-7

Home Theater
For Dummies,
3rd Edition
978-0-470-41189-6

Living the
Country Lifestyle
All-in-One
For Dummies
978-0-470-43061-3

Solar Power Your
Home
For Dummies,
2nd Edition
978-0-470-59678-4

Internet

Blogging For
Dummies,
3rd Edition
978-0-470-61996-4

eBay For Dummies,
6th Edition
978-0-470-49741-8

Facebook For
Dummies, 3rd Edition
978-0-470-87804-0

Web Marketing
For Dummies,
2nd Edition
978-0-470-37181-7

WordPress
For Dummies,
3rd Edition
978-0-470-59274-8

Language & Foreign Language

French For Dummies
978-0-7645-5193-2

Italian Phrases
For Dummies
978-0-7645-7203-6

Spanish For
Dummies, 2nd Edition
978-0-470-87855-2

Spanish For
Dummies, Audio Set
978-0-470-09585-0

Math & Science

Algebra I
For Dummies,
2nd Edition
978-0-470-55964-2

Biology
For Dummies,
2nd Edition
978-0-470-59875-7

Calculus For
Dummies
978-0-7645-2498-1

Chemistry For
Dummies
978-0-7645-5430-8

Microsoft Office

Excel 2010 For
Dummies
978-0-470-48953-6

Office 2010 All-in-One
For Dummies
978-0-470-49748-7

Office 2010 For
Dummies,
Book + DVD Bundle
978-0-470-62698-6

Word 2010 For
Dummies
978-0-470-48772-3

Music

Guitar For Dummies,
2nd Edition
978-0-7645-9904-0

iPod & iTunes
For Dummies,
8th Edition
978-0-470-87871-2

Piano Exercises
For Dummies
978-0-470-38765-8

Parenting & Education

Parenting For
Dummies,
2nd Edition
978-0-7645-5418-6

Type 1 Diabetes
For Dummies
978-0-470-17811-9

Pets

Cats For Dummies,
2nd Edition
978-0-7645-5275-5

Dog Training
For Dummies,
3rd Edition
978-0-470-60029-0

Puppies For
Dummies,
2nd Edition
978-0-470-03717-1

Religion & Inspiration

The Bible For
Dummies
978-0-7645-5296-0

Catholicism For
Dummies
978-0-7645-5391-2

Women in the Bible
For Dummies
978-0-7645-8475-6

Self-Help & Relationship

Anger Management
For Dummies
978-0-470-03715-7

Overcoming Anxiety
For Dummies,
2nd Edition
978-0-470-57441-6

Sports

Baseball
For Dummies,
3rd Edition
978-0-7645-7537-2

Basketball
For Dummies,
2nd Edition
978-0-7645-5248-9

Golf For Dummies,
3rd Edition
978-0-471-76871-5

Web Development

Web Design
All-in-One
For Dummies
978-0-470-41796-6

Web Sites
Do-It-Yourself
For Dummies,
2nd Edition
978-0-470-56520-9

Windows 7

Windows 7
For Dummies
978-0-470-49743-2

Windows 7
For Dummies,
Book + DVD Bundle
978-0-470-52398-8

Windows 7 All-in-One
For Dummies
978-0-470-48763-1

31901051970301